# Love
# Busters

## Other Books by Willard F. Harley, Jr.

# Love Busters

PROTECT Your Marriage
*by* Replacing Love-Busting Patterns
*with* LOVE-BUILDING HABITS

## Willard F. Harley, Jr.

Revell
*a division of Baker Publishing Group*
Grand Rapids, Michigan

© 1992, 1997, 2002, 2008, 2016 by Willard F. Harley, Jr.

Published by Revell
a division of Baker Publishing Group
P.O. Box 6287, Grand Rapids, MI 49516-6287
www.revellbooks.com

Printed in the United States of America

Library of Congress Cataloging-in-Publication Data is on file at the Library of Congress, Washington, DC.

ISBN 978-0-8007-2771-0

16   17   18   19   20   21   22        7   6   5   4   3   2   1

# Contents

# Contents

# Preface to the Revised
# & Updated *Love Busters*

It's been almost twenty-five years since I wrote *Love Busters* as a companion to my first book on marriage, *His Needs, Her Needs*. The reason that I chose this title, *Love Busters*, is that spouses often engage in habits that destroy their love for each other. If these habits are left to run amok, they will wreak havoc on a marriage.

While the primary focus of my first book, *His Needs, Her Needs*, was to teach couples how to *create* romantic love for each other, I wrote this companion, *Love Busters*, to teach them how to *avoid destroying* that love. At first you might think that destroying romantic love is simply failing to do what it takes to create it. But it turns out that the ways to create it and destroy it are entirely different.

As I explain in *His Needs, Her Needs*, spouses find fulfillment in marriage when their five most important emotional needs are met by each other. When that happens, romantic love is created and sustained. But in *Love Busters*, I identify six common habits of spouses that make each other miserable and destroy romantic love.

In the first half of my original *Love Busters* book, I presented the six Love Busters and what spouses could do to avoid them. Then, in the second half, I explained how couples could resolve common conflicts in marriage if they avoided using any of those Love Busters. But many readers felt that the first half did not provide enough help in learning how to overcome Love Busters.

So in this new book, I have expanded the first half to offer readers a more complete understanding of how to replace love-busting patterns with love-building habits. The information found in the second half of the original book—learning how to resolve common conflicts by not using Love Busters—is now found in another book I've written, *He Wins, She Wins*, and the accompanying *He Wins, She Wins Workbook*.

Although the title of this book is somewhat whimsical, there's nothing whimsical about Love Busters. They are extremely destructive to a marital relationship, and I've written this book to warn you of their threat to the love you and your spouse have for each other.

# 1

## The Secret to Lasting Love

When a couple first comes to my office, I talk with each of them separately. I've found that if they are together, they will spend most of their time criticizing each other. If I allow that to happen, they'll feel worse when the session is over than before they came. They would be engaging in Love Busters, which is one of the primary reasons they needed my help in the first place.

My practice of separating spouses during initial counseling sessions is based on a very important principle that I will repeat throughout this book. It's a point that I want you to fully understand:

Just about everything that you and your spouse do affects the way you feel about each other. What you do either builds your love for each other, or it destroys that love.

How spouses affect each other determines the success or failure of a marriage. If the spouses I'm counseling would simply stop doing the things that upset each other and start doing the things that make each other feel terrific, their marital problems would be over. Something else would happen too. They would be in love.

But even if they were to leave my office fully convinced that my basic principle is correct, the insight itself would not be enough to change the

*Just about everything that you and your spouse do affects the way you feel about each other. What you do either builds your love for each other, or it destroys that love.*

course of their marriage. They would both be required to follow through on that insight by making significant changes in their behavior. And those changes would be difficult for them to make. They would need a plan and a commitment to follow the plan until the changes were complete. But it would be worth making that effort because it would provide them with something that they both want—a fulfilling marriage.

### A Fulfilling Marriage Requires the Feeling of Love

Marriage is like an aircraft with exceptional performance—when it flies fast. But when it flies slowly, it cannot stay aloft—it stalls and crashes. When a husband and wife are in love with each other, they are happier, healthier, wiser, and more productive than ever. But when love fades, they lose everything that made them better people.

The feeling of love also gives a couple instinctive skills that make their marriage wonderful. They are more affectionate, conversant, and sexually attracted to each other than they would be if they were not in love. It almost seems like a miracle to those who experience it. But when they lose that love for each other, and those instinctive skills fade, what once seemed almost effortless becomes awkward and difficult. When that happens, a couple becomes disillusioned. *Why are we not caring for each other the way we once did?*

In an effort to force each other to provide the care they once took for granted, they become instinctively abusive and controlling. The instincts that once made a couple almost perfect for each other now change to make them so repulsive that they try to escape each other through divorce or permanent separation.

Take my word for it, because it's based on years of experience: If you want a marriage that satisfies both you and your spouse, you must be in love with each other. That's because once you lose the feeling of love in your marriage, it's a slippery slope all the way down to disliking or even hating each other. Instead of bringing out the best in each other, you will find yourselves bringing out the worst.

When a couple is first married, they think their feelings of love will last a lifetime. The vows and commitments they make depend on that assumption. But their passion for each other is usually short-lived. Some couples sustain it for just a few months or years after the wedding. For others, it's only days. And when passion leaves a marriage, the commitments usually leave along with it.

Some marriage counselors advise couples to accept the inevitable: Enjoy passion while it lasts but don't expect it to continue forever. Some recommend rising to a higher form of passionless love that they call "true love."

But I have found that couples do not have to accept the loss of love as inevitable. When spouses learn how to affect each other positively by meeting each other's emotional needs, and how to avoid affecting each other negatively, the love and passion they had when first married can be maintained throughout their marriage. My wife, Joyce, and I are among those who can honestly testify to having experienced continual love for each other throughout our fifty-four years of marriage because we have applied these important lessons to our lives.

But I have good news for couples who have experienced a loss of love: That love they once had for each other can be *restored*. And once it's back, all thoughts of passionless love, or even divorce, vanish.

*Impossible*, you may say. And it may certainly seem that way. When you're in love, it seems impossible that you will ever lose that feeling; and when you're out of love, it seems impossible to get it back. Most couples I counsel don't believe they will ever feel that love for each other again. But my methods for restoring passion do not require faith—they require action! When a couple follows my instructions, their love for each other returns.

## How to Fall in Love and Stay in Love

Let me return to the statement I made at the beginning of this chapter: *Just about everything that you and your spouse do affects the way you feel about each other. What you do either builds your love for each other, or it destroys that love.*

So the feeling of love in marriage is a litmus test of how you've been affecting each other. If you do what it takes to affect each other positively, and avoid affecting each other negatively, your passion for each other is the result.

I've written two books to help you create and sustain your feeling of love. They work together. While the first book, *His Needs, Her Needs,* helps you *build* the feeling of love, this book, *Love Busters,* helps you avoid *losing* that love.

You create the feeling of love for each other by doing what it takes to make each other feel terrific—by meeting each other's most important emotional needs. *His Needs, Her Needs* teaches you how to identify those needs and then meet them throughout your lives together. But even if you meet each other's emotional needs, you can destroy the love that meeting those needs creates if you tolerate habits that I call Love Busters. If Love Busters exist in your marriage, sustained love doesn't have a chance.

The lessons of this book will teach you how to throw those rascals out. I'll help you identify them and explain how you can overcome them. Once they're gone and you're meeting each other's emotional needs, you'll have lasting love.

I encourage you and your spouse to nurture the feeling of love you have for each other. It's not only a test of how you are affecting each other; it's also the ultimate criterion for how well you're caring for each other. But if you have lost your passion, don't despair. It can be restored to your marriage if you follow my advice. And once it is restored, you'll agree that it is too valuable to ever lose again.

# 2

## The Love Bank

Since so much personal and familial happiness depends on the success of marriage, you'd think that couples would approach their relationship with a careful plan to ensure success. But sadly, most don't give their marriages much thought until it's almost too late. About half of all marriages end in divorce, and most of the others are a bitter disappointment. Very few marriages, about 20 percent, or 1 in 5, turn out to be as fulfilling as couples hoped they would be.

I'd like your marriage to be one of these exceptions. I've written this book, and its companion, *His Needs, Her Needs*, to help you avoid the tragedy of a divorce, or even an unfulfilling marriage. I'd like to show you how to build a happy marriage that *stays* happy. If you are still in love, my advice will help you stay in love. But if you've already lost some of the passion you once had for each other, I'd like to help you recover it in a spectacular way. My recommendations have helped millions of couples replace marital pain with marital pleasure, and you can be one of them.

In most marriages, the love a couple once had for each other eventually turns to apathy, or even hate. How does that happen? It's something you must fully understand if you want to avoid that experience.

To help you understand the rise and fall of the feeling of love, I've invented a concept that I call the **Love Bank**. It also helps me explain how a couple can restore their feeling of love for each other after it's been lost.

Within all of us is a Love Bank that contains **accounts** in the names of all of the people we know. It keeps track of the way people treat us. When someone does something that makes us feel good, **love units** are **deposited** into their account. And when that person does something that makes us feel bad, love units are **withdrawn**. If someone makes us feel good more often than they make us feel bad, that person builds a positive Love Bank balance. If, on the other hand, he or she tends to make us feel bad more often, they end up with a negative balance.

Our emotions check our Love Bank regularly to determine who is affecting us positively and who isn't. With that evidence, they encourage us to spend more time with those with positive balances by making them **attractive** to us. On the other hand, our emotions encourage us to avoid people who have negative balances by making those people feel **repulsive**. We have very little control over these feelings, and they are based almost entirely on Love Bank balances. We like people with positive balances and dislike those with negative balances.

Once in a while, someone of the opposite sex comes along who makes us feel absolutely sensational. That's because they meet one or more of our most important emotional needs. (I explain what the most important emotional needs are, and how you can identify them for yourselves, in chapter 16.)

When that happens, so many love units are deposited that his or her account breaks through what I call the **romantic love threshold**. Our emotions are so impressed with that high balance that they give us added incentive to spend more time with that person: they give us the feeling of love—**romantic love**. We don't merely find that person attractive. We find that person irresistible! And along with that feeling goes a desire to spend our lives with whoever has that high Love Bank balance. Marriage is an easy choice when Love Bank balances are above the romantic love threshold.

That's how you probably felt when you were first married. You were in love. You met each other's most important emotional needs so effectively while dating that your Love Bank balances breached the romantic love threshold. Once in love, you couldn't imagine being apart—or out of love with each other.

## What Goes Up, Can Go Down

Before marriage, while a couple is dating, they usually try to deposit a tremendous number of love units by doing things that make each other very happy—they want to meet each other's emotional needs. They also try to avoid doing whatever might make each other unhappy. If they fail to please each other and fail to avoid hurting each other, their relationship doesn't usually make it to the altar. It's usually only those who find each other irresistible who want to be together for the rest of their lives.

But unfortunately, after marriage most couples fail to keep their Love Bank balances above the romantic love threshold. Their new responsibilities of life prevent them from doing as good a job meeting each other's emotional needs. And they begin doing things that are annoying and selfish. They don't try as hard to be thoughtful as they did before marriage. When that happens they lose their feeling of love for each other.

But it gets worse. When a couple loses their romantic love for each other, the instincts that made it easy for them to meet each other's emotional needs while in love seem to disappear. Now they don't feel like meeting those needs as they did before. And that failure to meet those needs makes it tempting to become controlling and abusive in order to get the job done; this is when spouses try to force each other to meet those needs.

*It's not uncommon for a couple who started out feeling that they would love each other forever to come to the conclusion that their marriage was the biggest mistake of their lives.*

Such tactics not only fail to help spouses achieve their goal, but they also drive Love Bank balances below zero. What had been a feeling of attraction turns into a feeling of repulsion. It's not uncommon for a couple who started out feeling that they would love each other forever to come to the conclusion that their marriage was the biggest mistake of their lives.

And it's all due to Love Bank balances. If a couple can simply keep their Love Bank balances above the romantic love threshold, they would have a marriage full of passion for the rest of their lives. But because they allow their balances to drop below that threshold, they lose their feeling of love for each other. And then in a misguided effort to address the problem they often hurt each other, driving their Love Bank balances into negative territory.

## Marriage Can Make Us Hate the One We Once Loved

Of all the people you know, you are more likely to hate your spouse than anyone else. And your spouse is more likely to hate you than anyone else. Since you may not believe me or may think I am exaggerating, I will use the Love Bank analogy to help me explain to you why this is such a common experience in marriage.

Most of our personal relationships are voluntary. That is, we choose those we spend time with and they choose us. And the primary basis for that choice is usually how we feel about that person which, in turn, depends on their Love Bank balances. Those people with positive balances feel attractive to us, so we want to spend time with them. The more deposits they make, the more we like them and the more we choose to be with them.

On the other hand, our emotions encourage us to avoid those whose Love Bank accounts are in the red. These are the people who make us unhappy. So by avoiding these people, we prevent them from making even more withdrawals. Since we don't give them an opportunity to withdraw as many love units as they might, we usually don't dislike these people very much—we "close their account" before things get that bad.

But there are some people who are not easy to avoid. At work, at home, in our churches, clubs, or community activities, we have to deal with certain people whether we like them or not. And these are the ones we can grow to hate, because we give them an opportunity to keep making Love Bank withdrawals until their account reaches the

**hate threshold.** That's the negative balance that our emotions use to trigger an intense feeling of **repulsion** toward someone who has consistently and repeatedly made us unhappy. Just as our emotions give us added incentive (the feeling of incredible attraction) to be with those with accounts over the romantic love threshold, our emotions give us added incentive (the feeling of incredible repulsion) to avoid those with accounts under the hate threshold.

You might find another job or switch churches to avoid someone who treats you badly enough. Uncles, aunts, cousins, and other members of your extended family can be avoided, at least for most of the year. With greater effort it is possible to avoid brothers and sisters, or even parents.

But a spouse is almost impossible to avoid, especially if you have children, unless you separate or divorce. So it should come as no surprise that the person in the best position to make massive withdrawals from their account in your Love Bank is your spouse. And you are in the best position to make massive withdrawals from your account in your spouse's Love Bank. For that reason, you and your spouse are more likely to hate each other than anyone else. You are each other's hardest person to avoid—regardless of how miserable you make each other feel.

Day after day, month after month, year after year, you and your spouse can withdraw love units by making demands of each other, criticizing each other, being angry with each other, lying to each other, engaging in thoughtless activities, and annoying each other with disgusting habits. And what can you do about it? What can you do to get each other to stop?

You do what most people do: Dish it back as fast as it comes. If you're miserable, then, by golly, you'll *both* be miserable. Your instinct is to destroy the one who is upsetting you, and almost all couples respond that way when Love Bank accounts fall into the red.

When a married couple's relationship starts on a downward slide, Love Bank withdrawals usually gain momentum. Instead of caring for each other, spouses devise increasingly painful strategies to pay each other back for the last thoughtless act. As negative Love Bank balances increase, the feeling of anger and disrespect increases. Because they live together, a couple cannot avoid each other, and withdrawals continue unabated. The end result is often the violence that comes from a deep and pervasive hatred.

By that time, their only choice seems to be either a divorce or to have as little to do with each other as possible. They give up on trying to care for each other, and decide instead to ignore each other and live as independently as possible. While that may minimize Love Bank withdrawals, it makes marital fulfillment impossible. They give up on ever having the marriage that they had once hoped to have.

*All the best intentions, sincere vows, and honest efforts cannot substitute for a substantial Love Bank account.*

The best way to avoid this tragedy, of course, is to keep Love Bank balances above the romantic love threshold. Or, if they fall below that threshold, or even fall into the negative range, do what it takes to bring those balances back up again. And what it takes, of course, is to affect each other positively and avoid affecting each other negatively.

All the best intentions, sincere vows, and honest efforts cannot substitute for a substantial Love Bank account. The Love Bank determines who we marry and it usually determines whether or not we'll be divorced. Therefore it is tremendously important to understand how to build Love Bank accounts and how to avoid withdrawals once deposits have been made.

## What Are Love Busters?

Whenever you do something that upsets your spouse, you make a Love Bank withdrawal. But let's face it, it's impossible to avoid all the bumps and bruises of life, especially *marital* bumps and bruises. Even in the best marriages, spouses hurt each other now and then.

But occasional mistakes do not drain a Love Bank as long as they're seen as mistakes. An apology quickly heals the wound if the offense is not committed again.

It's when a mistake turns into a habit, repeated again and again, that Love Bank balances are at great risk of falling. In these situations, apologies mean very little because the same mistake keeps being made. Nothing is done to keep love units from flowing out of the Love Bank.

I call these **habits** that drain the Love Bank **Love Busters**, because they do more to ruin romantic love than anything else.

Through years of marriage counseling, I've been made aware of a host of Love Busters, but each one falls into one of six categories:

1. Selfish Demands
2. Disrespectful Judgments
3. Angry Outbursts
4. Dishonesty
5. Independent Behavior
6. Annoying Habits

The first three categories of Love Busters—selfish demands, disrespectful judgments, and angry outbursts—all have something in common with each other. They are ways that spouses try to control each other. And they're intentionally harmful: a spouse knows that when he or she engages in one of those Love Busters there will be a Love Bank withdrawal.

But the remaining three Love Busters—dishonesty, independent behavior, and annoying habits—are not always intentionally harmful to your spouse. As you will see, dishonesty can be your way of protecting your spouse from unpleasant information; you are usually not even thinking about your spouse when you engage in independent behavior; and annoying habits can be so automatic that they occur without your even being aware that you're doing them. But being unintentional doesn't make them any less damaging to Love Bank balances. In fact, in the long run they may actually cause more withdrawals than the three intentional ones.

Because each of these six categories of Love Busters is so important, I will discuss them one at a time in the following chapters and show you not only how to overcome each of them, but also how to replace them with a love builder.

In marriage you have an unprecedented opportunity to make your spouse happy. You do that whenever you meet his or her most important emotional needs. But you are also in a position to make your spouse miserable, more miserable than anyone else can make them.

In too many marriages, spouses make each other miserable. When they come to me with their marital problems, my ultimate goal is to teach them how to make each other happy. But before I can get to that goal, I must often first teach them how to stop hurting each other.

So even though *His Needs, Her Needs* was the first book I wrote to help create fulfilling marriages, in actual practice, I usually begin by helping couples overcome their Love Busters. That's because there's no point in making Love Bank deposits if they drain out faster than they're deposited.

*Of everyone on earth, you have the greatest opportunity to make your spouse miserable, and unless you consciously and deliberately avoid these six Love Busters, you will become your spouse's source of greatest unhappiness.*

Of everyone on earth, you have the greatest opportunity to make your spouse miserable, and unless you consciously and deliberately avoid these six Love Busters, you will become your spouse's source of greatest unhappiness.

By the time you finish this book, you will know how to protect each other from yourselves. By overcoming Love Busters, you'll be able to plug up the leaks in your Love Bank accounts so that when you make deposits, they will accumulate until you are passionately in love with each other—essential for a happy and fulfilling marriage. Once you learn these lessons, your efforts to meet each other's emotional needs will reap huge dividends. The Love Bank deposits you make will break through the romantic love threshold, and you'll be in love with each other again.

## Key Principles

Just about everything that you and your spouse do affects the way you feel about each other. What you do either builds your love for each other, or it destroys that love.

All of us have within us a **Love Bank** that keeps track of the way people treat us. When someone does something that makes us feel good, **love units** are **deposited** into their **account**. And when he or she does something that makes us feel bad, love units are **withdrawn**.

Our emotions check our Love Bank regularly to determine who is taking care of us and who isn't. With that evidence, they encourage us to spend more time with those who have positive balances by making them **attractive** to us, and to avoid those who have negative balances by making them **repulsive**.

When someone of the opposite sex makes us feel sensational by meeting one or more of our basic emotional needs, so many love units are deposited that his or her account balance breaks through the **romantic love threshold**. Our emotions are so impressed with that high balance that they give us added incentive to spend as much time as possible with that person—they give us the feeling of **romantic love**. We don't merely find that person attractive—we find that person irresistible.

Our emotions encourage us to avoid those whose Love Bank accounts are in the red. But some people, like our spouse, are not easy to avoid, so they may keep withdrawing love units until their account reaches the **hate threshold**. When that happens, we find that person incredibly repulsive.

Just as our emotions give us added incentive (the feeling of love) to be with those with accounts over the romantic love threshold, our emotions give us added incentive (the feeling of hate) to avoid those with accounts under the hate threshold.

It's not uncommon for a couple that started out feeling that they would love each other for eternity to come to the conclusion that their marriage was the biggest mistake of their lives. And it's all due to Love Bank balances.

**Love Busters** are **habits** that drain the Love Bank. They fall into six categories: **selfish demands, disrespectful judgments, angry outbursts, dishonesty, independent behavior,** and **annoying habits.** The first three are intentional (spouses do them knowing that they will hurt each other) and the final three are usually unintentional (they are not usually done to deliberately hurt each other).

Of everyone on earth, you have the greatest opportunity to make your spouse miserable, and unless you consciously and deliberately avoid these six Love Busters, you will become your spouse's source of greatest unhappiness.

## *Consider This . . .*

1. Try to explain the Love Bank to each other in your own words. Most couples have trouble discussing Love Bank withdrawals, because it often sounds like criticism. How could you let each other know about withdrawals that are taking place in a constructive way?

2. There are many who believe that the feeling of love cannot be sustained in marriage. What do you think? If you believe that it can be sustained, is it important enough for both of you to do whatever it takes to keep your Love Bank balances above the romantic love threshold?

3. How do Love Bank balances affect your willingness to meet each other's emotional needs? How do they affect your temptation to hurt each other? When your Love Bank balances are negative, what should you try to do for each other that you don't feel like doing? What do you feel like doing to each other that you should avoid doing?

4. What are Love Busters? Why do I emphasize habits rather than isolated behaviors?

# 3

## How Love Busters
## Can Wreck a Marriage

Karen couldn't even remember what it was like being in love with Jim. Whenever he was home, her stomach knotted up and she often felt sick. When they talked, which wasn't very often, she was usually defensive. Vacationing together was unthinkable—if she wanted to relax, he had to be far away. Could she survive this marriage long enough for her children to grow up? Her marriage was looking increasingly hopeless to her.

When I talked with Karen for the first time, she wanted a separation from Jim, one that would help her survive a few more years of their marriage. Their youngest daughter, Lisa, was thirteen. For Lisa's sake, Karen wanted to wait five or six years before divorcing Jim.

You may not be feeling as desperate as Karen felt that day, but you may have experienced something of what she was going through—the fighting, the sarcasm, the disrespect, and the loneliness.

But marriage isn't supposed to be like that. It should be a caring relationship, where a husband and wife treat each other with kindness and patience, not with rudeness and anger.

Karen had expected Jim to care for her in an extraordinary way. And while she was dating him, she had no reason to expect anything else. He talked with her almost every day, focusing his attention on what

23

he could do to help her, and he was always there for her whenever she had a problem. He even changed his plans whenever they conflicted with her plans.

Arguments? They didn't have any, because Jim was usually willing to try to see things from her perspective. Again and again he proved to Karen that caring for her was his highest priority—and that made her feel loved and very secure.

## Jim's Neglect

While dating, it was relatively easy to resolve conflicts that Jim and Karen faced because their lives were not very complicated. But not long after their wedding, Karen was pregnant and wanted to work fewer hours after their child arrived. Jim assumed that his income had to increase to make up the difference, so he decided to work longer hours. He began to feel the financial pressure of becoming a family man. Their lives had become very stressful and their conflicts were more difficult to resolve.

With more of his time and energy spent at work, Jim's ability to meet Karen's emotional needs eroded. During her pregnancy, when she needed his emotional support more than ever, he expected her to work things out on her own. Instead of making her the love of his life and center of his attention, he seemed to cut her adrift. At least that's how Karen felt about the way he treated her.

But from Jim's perspective, his neglect made sense. *After all*, he thought, *we're both intelligent adults. She can take the car to the garage just as easily as I can. Why should she expect me to drop everything at work to do something she can do for herself? Am I her servant? Is she a princess?*

At first, Karen was deeply troubled by his change of attitude, though she tried not to show it. She made a valiant effort to accommodate his new approach to their relationship, troubleshooting around the home, rearranging her schedule to fit his, but when she was alone, she cried. *Why has he changed so much? Is it because I'm pregnant? Am I ugly?*

By the time little Andrea arrived, Karen's earlier conviction that Jim cared for her had been seriously damaged. He had not only failed to support her during pregnancy, but he made matters worse by having little to do with Andrea after her birth. He was so focused on becoming a success at work that he had become a failure at home. Karen felt utterly abandoned. *Maybe*, she thought, *he no longer loves me.*

## Karen's Neglect

As the chemistry of their relationship deteriorated, Karen's care for Jim deteriorated along with it. In response to Jim's neglect of her, Karen began to neglect him. She no longer asked him how his day went; she didn't show him much affection or admiration anymore; and she wasn't very enthusiastic about making love either.

Jim didn't pay much attention to the fact that Karen had stopped being affectionate or that she wasn't as admiring. But he sure noticed her loss of sexual interest. When they were first married, she had looked forward to making love to him, and was very passionate whenever she did. Now she tried to avoid it. Whenever they made love, she felt used.

One day Jim got up the courage to ask her what was going on. "Karen, what's happening to you? Why do you keep pushing me away?"

"I'm sorry, Jim," she replied. "I just haven't been in the mood lately. I don't know why."

There were a host of common excuses that she could have used. After a child's birth the mother is usually exhausted much of the time, and sex requires energy. She could have used that as an excuse. Or she could have focused attention on the fact that Andrea took away their privacy. But deep down, she knew that her loss of sexual interest was directly related to Jim's neglect.

But Jim thought he was doing what was expected of him in marriage. His new family needed his financial support, and he kept telling Karen that he was giving her as much of his time as he could afford. So she felt that there was no point in discussing it. What was there to discuss? Why even mention his neglect?

"What do you think it would take to get you in the mood?" It was difficult for Jim to raise the subject. He felt like he was begging.

But Karen wasn't making it easy for him, either. "I don't know," she answered. "I just don't know."

The truth was that Jim had stopped doing the things that made Karen fall in love with him. He was not as supportive, not as accommodating, and worst of all, he spent very little time alone with her. Her emotional needs were not being met anymore. Consequently, she felt emotionally disconnected from him. Sex, it turned out, was something she felt like doing only when she knew that Jim loved and cared for her. It was then that she felt bonded to him—emotionally one. But now she was feeling emotionally neglected, so what had been effortless became very difficult for her.

While Jim and Karen were dating, they often expressed their feeling of love for each other. That's because those feelings were so strong, they could hardly avoid mentioning it. But when Karen's passion for Jim began to erode, she didn't warn him. In fact, she kept telling him she loved him, when deep down she knew her feelings were changing. Her married friends told her that loss of passion in marriage was something she had to expect. After all, they said, passion was for newlyweds, not for couples who become parents. So Karen focused her attention away from Jim, and toward Andrea. Her daughter became her highest priority in life.

## No Problem-Solving Skills

From the beginning of their marriage, Jim and Karen had rarely discussed the growing problems with their relationship. When one offended the other, it was usually ignored. But now they had a problem they could not ignore so easily—or at least Jim could not ignore. He didn't want to go through life with a sexually reluctant wife and he didn't know how to fix the problem.

Jim's primary mistake was to make the unilateral decision that his career obligations were more important than meeting Karen's emotional needs. It's one of the Love Busters that we will be discussing in this book—**independent behavior**. He made career decisions without asking Karen how she felt about them and how they affected her. He made those decisions as if she didn't exist.

Karen's primary mistake was to give Jim misleading information about how his neglect was affecting her. That's another Love Buster—**dishonesty**.

Those two mistakes, independent behavior and dishonesty, helped create a cascade of events, and other Love Busters, that almost led to their divorce.

Had Jim made his work-related decisions jointly with Karen, and had Karen given Jim accurate feedback regarding how she was reacting to his behavior, they would have known how to resolve their sexual problems. He would have gone back to doing what had drawn her to him in the beginning, cheerfully helping her whenever she had a problem, accommodating her in his schedule, and now that Andrea had joined them, taking an active role in the care of their new daughter. Sexual problems solved!

> *Those two mistakes, independent behavior and dishonesty, helped create a cascade of events, and other Love Busters, that almost led to their divorce.*

But Jim and Karen didn't understand how his unilateral decisions and her dishonesty prevented them from solving their sexual problem. And with it unsolved, Jim's frustration introduced a new and destructive chapter in their marriage. He felt he had no choice. He had to force the issue.

**The Road to Marital Disaster**

One night, after Jim and Karen had gone to bed, he reached over to try to initiate lovemaking. Knowing what he was up to, she pushed him away. Jim's feelings of resentment had been building for some time and her rejection sent him over the edge.

"I've had enough of this!" Jim blurted out.

"Quiet, you'll wake Andrea."

"Why don't you ever want to make love to me? What's the matter with you?"

"We'll talk about this in the morning. Please, go to sleep," Karen pleaded.

"Not this time," Jim shouted. "I need to have sex with you, and I need it now!"

Karen tried to get out of bed, but Jim grabbed her arm. She pulled herself free and tried to get out of the room, but Jim blocked the door.

Afraid he would hit her, she huddled in a corner of the room not daring to say a word.

Jim was furious. He called her names and lectured her for what seemed to Karen to be an eternity. All his pent-up resentment poured out in a moment of unrestrained rage.

When it was over, Jim felt much better. He had finally said what he had felt for such a long time. But Karen was upset beyond words. He started to apologize for losing his temper but then stopped himself. *I'm glad I had the courage to say what I felt*, he thought. *Now we're getting somewhere!*

They were getting somewhere all right, but not where Jim wanted to go. They were now on the road to marital disaster.

Jim put his arm around Karen, telling her how much he loved her. Still in the corner, she didn't dare push him away now. All she could do was cry. As he became more amorous, she let him do anything he wanted—eventually they made love. Jim felt it was one of their best sexual experiences ever. Karen felt raped.

That evening, Jim ruined his marriage by using three Love Busters. It began with **selfish demands** when he demanded sex from Karen, giving her no right to refuse. When she resisted his demand, he used **disrespectful judgments** to berate her for her unwillingness. Then he had an **angry outburst** in an effort to force her to make love to him.

Many women would have gone straight to an attorney the next day to end the marriage, but Karen believed she had too much to lose to go it alone with a small child. So after she had time to reflect on the nightmare she had experienced, she made some decisions that she thought would help her survive.

First, she would never be found cowering in a corner again. Next time he lost his temper she would fight fire with fire—let him know what a creep she thought he had become.

Second, she would learn to become emotionally independent of Jim so she wouldn't be so vulnerable. She had already been doing almost everything without him, but she had hoped that some day they would return to the passion they once had for each other. But now she was convinced that her only hope for survival was to create an independent life of her own that was completely separate from his.

Karen made one huge concession, however. What made him so angry was his unmet need for sex, so she decided to accommodate him. She felt it was her duty as long as they were married.

At first, Jim thought his prayers had been answered. Whenever he wanted sex, he got it. And Karen seemed more passionate. For the first week they made love every night.

But Karen had erected an emotional barrier around herself that Jim couldn't penetrate. Whenever Karen received help from him, even when he did what she wanted, she gave him no credit. Furthermore, she didn't let him do anything that would meet her most important emotional needs, like being affectionate or talking to him about her deepest feelings, because that would make her too emotionally vulnerable.

Instead, Karen demanded freedom to do whatever she pleased. She spent more money on herself and she was with her friends during most of her leisure time. She began to think that, as a wife and mother, she had forgotten to care for herself all these years. So her own personal interests came in a very close second to those of Andrea. Jim's interests, with the exception of sex, were near the bottom of her list.

Karen scheduled her week without any input from Jim. She encouraged him to leave for work early and come home late. If he planned to be home for the weekend, she would plan to do something with her friends. She did not even deposit her own check into their joint account. The money she earned went into her own separate account and she made Jim pay all their bills.

Though Jim now had no sexual complaints, he was still frustrated much of the time. He was particularly upset with Karen's failure to let him know where she was going or what she had been doing. And he didn't like the way she kept her income separate from his and her spending a secret. Whenever he asked about her schedule or the money she was spending, she told him it was none of his business. When he argued with her about her secrecy, she would scream at him to leave her alone. If he persisted, she would threaten to leave him. That was usually effective in backing him off.

Jim might have been willing to suffer through the bad marriage for the rest of his life if Karen had kept making love to him regularly. But her commitment didn't last very long. At first, she allowed herself to say no once in a while, but within a few months she was saying no almost every time.

Actually, Karen's commitment to lovemaking was poorly conceived. In the beginning, her lovemaking had been an enjoyable expression of her love for Jim. When she lost that love due to his neglect, it wasn't so enjoyable anymore, so she had resisted it. But now that she was hating him, lovemaking became almost impossible for her. Since none of us can force ourselves to do something that's terribly unpleasant indefinitely, she eventually couldn't force herself to make love to Jim anymore. Her stomach knotted up at the very thought of it.

The brief reprieve that had been brought on by frequent lovemaking came to an end. Jim and Karen were left with nothing that made their marriage enjoyable and everything that made it a nightmare. By the time they made their first appointment with me, they could hardly remember what it was like being in love.

### I Can't Take This Anymore!

Jim and Karen's experience is all too common in today's marriages. What begins as a caring and thoughtful relationship turns sour when a couple, often very innocently, fails to meet each other's emotional needs. Their inability to solve that problem the right way leads them to make two disastrous mistakes. First, they try to force each other to meet their emotional needs by being abusive and controlling, and second, when that doesn't work, they create independent lifestyles, keeping themselves separated from each other as much as possible. When these mistakes are made, their love turns into hate. Love Busters have ruined their marriage.

Some couples try to suffer through it for the sake of their children or their religious convictions. But most often, they decide that they can't take it anymore—they file for divorce. Unfortunately, divorce doesn't usually ease the pain. All exits lead to disaster for the couple and their family.

## Key Principles

While dating, conflicts are relatively easy to resolve to both partners' satisfaction because they are not very complicated. But after marriage, especially after children arrive and conflicts become more complicated, couples are tempted to use Love Busters to resolve them.

Jim's primary mistake was in making unilateral decisions regarding his career (independent behavior), failing to take Karen's interests into account. Then, when his emotional needs were not being met by Karen because he was failing to meet hers, he made further mistakes by using the following Love Busters: selfish demands, disrespectful judgments, and angry outbursts.

Karen's primary mistake was in failing to give Jim her honest reactions (dishonesty) to how his career decisions were affecting her and how she reacted to his demands, disrespect, and anger when he wanted her to make love to him more often. Then she compounded her first mistake by making another mistake in trying to live as if her husband didn't exist (independent behavior).

Jim and Karen's use of Love Busters in their effort to resolve their conflicts almost led to their divorce.

## Consider This . . .

1. Before you read the next chapter, I encourage you to discuss the tragic events of Jim and Karen's marriage. Are there any similarities between their marriage and yours?

2. If you had been advising Jim and Karen during the first year of their marriage, what would you have suggested to them? Would that same advice help your marriage?

# 4

## Selfish Demands: *Part 1*

### Who Wants to Live with a Dictator?

In an effort to provide for his new family, Jim spent so much time at work that he had neglected to meet Karen's emotional needs. It was an innocent mistake, but it led to her loss of emotional connection to him, which, in turn, caused her to lose interest in sex. That was a serious problem for Jim, and he didn't know how to solve it.

Karen didn't help. Instead of telling him what was bothering her, she claimed not to understand the problem herself. In response to his frustration, Jim made an almost fatal mistake—he demanded sex. As a result of this fateful course of action, his relationship with Karen took such a nosedive that it almost crashed. His demand for sex not only failed to address their underlying problems, but it eventually brought their lovemaking to a complete stop.

Jim and Karen's struggle with sex is fairly common in marriage, so many couples can relate somewhat to this opening illustration. But with the possibility that your sexual relationship is okay, I'll introduce another example in this chapter to describe the inappropriateness of demands in marriage. You may have experienced something similar to this—possibly last week.

Imagine yourself cleaning up after dinner with your kitchen a mess, your kids running wild, and your husband watching TV (if you are a husband, imagine how you might feel being the wife in this situation). You are feeling very neglected and wonder how he could sit there so oblivious to your need for help. At the very least, you think, he could offer to calm the children down or dry the dishes. But instead he is just sitting there while a myriad of things need to be done.

Out of utter frustration, you walk up to the TV, turn it off, point your finger at your husband, and say, "I'm giving you a choice: you can either watch the children for me or you can clean up the kitchen, but you are *not* watching television."

If you can identify with this situation, you might consider this approach to the problem both courageous and wise. By taking control, the job will get done and the husband will be doing something that he should have volunteered to do in the first place, you might reason. But if you have ever been on the receiving end of such a demand, you can probably see the fly in this ointment.

## Demands Seem Reasonable . . .

If you command your spouse to do something for you that benefits you at your spouse's expense, you are guilty of making a **selfish demand**. But at the time, you probably don't think that what you are doing is selfish or demanding. It seems reasonable when you're frustrated and your spouse isn't cooperating. Most spouses make demands when they don't know what else to do.

> *If you command your spouse to do something for you that benefits you at your spouse's expense, you are guilty of making a selfish demand.*

Think for a moment about how you and your spouse ask each other for favors. Do you tell each other what to do, as if one of you is a sergeant and the other a private? Or do you ask each other with a willingness to take no for an answer?

Because you care about each other in marriage, you're tempted to assume that your spouse should make you happy, and so you're simply telling your spouse how to do something that he or she should want to do. After all, you've been trying to do whatever makes your spouse happy, haven't you? But if you find that your spouse is being negligent in his or her duties, a little nudge in the right direction seems very appropriate.

However, even if it seems reasonable at the time, when you tell each other what to do, you're making a demand. It's an insidious habit that, if left to run amok, can destroy your ability to solve your marital conflicts—and destroy your love for each other.

As soon as children begin to talk, demands become part of their vocabulary when they're frustrated. They must be taught by their parents to make requests rather than demands, regardless of how frustrated they may be. But in marriage, all of that training seems to go down the drain. Even though you probably don't make demands of any adult other than your spouse, you assume that it's okay to do so in your marriage. You don't see the damage that it does. And even if you know deep down that your spouse doesn't like your demands, you may not know any other way to communicate your frustration.

When spouses make demands, they usually feel that the end justifies the means. While it might cause some unhappiness, they're simply trying to make their spouse do the right thing. And doing what's right is more important than being happy.

When Jim demanded sex of Karen, he wanted her to fulfill her responsibilities to him. From her perspective, however, the demand turned lovemaking into rape.

A husband should fulfill his wife's demand for help in the kitchen after dinner, shouldn't he? How else can she get the help she needs? But the husband will not think of it as her cry for help. He'll see it as her attempt to control him.

None of us wants to be bossed around, even when it means helping someone we love. Instead of being told what to do, we want our help to be requested. And yet, it seems so unnatural to request help, when you feel so certain that you deserve it.

Your frustration begins on your ride home from work. You are exhausted from a full day of preparing insurance claims, yet you face an evening of even more work caring for your husband and children.

*Why should I be responsible for all this work*, you're thinking to yourself. *He expects me to do everything. He spends a leisurely evening at home while I'm working myself to exhaustion. Is that fair?*

Upon arrival at home you keep thinking, *He doesn't even tell me when he's coming home from work. He expects me to have dinner ready for him. He expects the kids to be cared for and he doesn't even have the decency to call me and let me know when he's coming home.*

When your husband arrives home, he says "hi" to the kids that come rushing to him at the door. And instead of acknowledging you right away, he turns on the television. Eventually he gets around to greeting you and gives you a peck on the cheek.

Now you're thinking, *Is that the only reward he can think of for all the work I've done? He's expecting me to be his slave!*

### . . . But Demands Are Abusive and Controlling

**Abuse** in marriage is the *deliberate attempt of a spouse to cause the other to be unhappy.* So demands are a form of verbal abuse, because they certainly do cause unhappiness and they are made with intent.

> *Demands are abusive because they cause unhappiness and they are made with intent. Demands are controlling because they are made with the purpose of forcing a spouse to do something against their will.*

Demands are also **controlling** because they are made with the purpose of forcing a spouse to do something against their will. Those who have been the target of demands in marriage know that they are being controlled, and they resent it.

It's not fair for you to do all the work at home after a hard day at the office. You should be relieved of some of those responsibilities. But I object to the way you are trying to solve the problem. You want change, and I would agree that a change is in order. But the way you are going about achieving that change is abusive and controlling. It doesn't take your husband's feelings into account. That's because you don't care how your husband feels about helping you—he should be helping regardless of how he feels!

36

*But wait a minute*, you might be thinking. *I'm not demanding that he do all the work. I'm demanding only that he share in the work, which is his responsibility. I'll still be doing my fair share.*

I sympathize with that reasoning. You may think that your solution is fair because it works for you. But it's only fair when both of you think it's fair. You're in no position to determine your husband's interests—they should be determined by him.

A fair solution to any marital problem must take both of your interests into account. You must somehow solve the problem of getting the help you need in a way that makes you both happy. That solution is the one that is most likely to become a permanent solution, and once it's permanent, it will reinforce your love for each other. That solution will help make deposits into both of your Love Banks every day.

If your solution to a marital problem makes only you happy, it won't work in the long run, and it will erode the love that your unhappy spouse has for you. And even if you get your way by making demands, you won't be happy in the long run because of the effort it takes to keep trying to force your spouse to get the job done. If you want to be in love and stay in love, it makes a lot more sense to make lifestyle choices that work well for both of you.

## Win-Lose Conflict Resolution Strategies in Marriage

When a conflict is resolved with both spouses happy with the outcome, it's a win-win resolution. But couples tend to settle for win-lose resolutions right from the beginning of their relationship. While dating, each partner tends to use the **sacrifice strategy** when there's a conflict: They sacrifice their own interests to make each other happy. If she wants to shop, he goes with her even though he really doesn't like shopping. If he wants to fish, she goes with him even if she doesn't like fishing. Other conflicts are resolved in a similar way by agreeing to each other's wishes. When a couple sacrifices for each other, they don't let each other know that one is losing so the other can win. Instead, they give the impression that they enjoy what they are doing. There is not a hint of reluctance.

Then after they are married, they usually modify the sacrifice strategy with one change: They are honest about their reactions. He explains that he really doesn't enjoy shopping, and she lets him know that she doesn't enjoy fishing. But they still expect each other to join in on those activities. And when they express a desire, they expect the other person to fulfill it as an act of care. After all, isn't losing so that the other person can win the ultimate way of expressing care?

This change in the sacrifice strategy is called the **capitulation strategy**, which is like sacrifice in that one spouse willingly loses so that the other can win. But unlike sacrifice, which is usually given without any expression of reluctance, a spouse that capitulates lets the other know that they are the loser.

For a while, capitulation as an approach to conflict resolution may work, but as life becomes more challenging it becomes more apparent that it does not work. Spouses become less willing to give in when increasingly complicated conflicts that every married couple faces arise, especially when children arrive.

## Dictatorship

In many marriages, when conflicts seem to be irresolvable to both spouses' satisfaction, one spouse will decide that he or she must make the "final" decisions. They begin to use the **dictator strategy** whenever a conflict arises. This strategy assumes that one spouse has the right, wisdom, and compassion to make decisions correctly. While the other spouse can lobby to have their interests taken into account, when a decision is made, it's final.

If a spouse is a benevolent dictator, truly wise and compassionate, the dictator strategy can work in marriage. By understanding the other spouse's feelings and interests, choices are made that are mutually advantageous.

But dictators haven't been known to be particularly wise or compassionate. They tend to make decisions in their own interest and at the expense of their citizens. And the same thing happens in marriage. When one spouse is given the right to make all final decisions, the other spouse usually suffers. And their love suffers with each selfish decision.

Selfish demands prevail in most marriages when the dictator strategy is in force—one spouse telling the other what to do without coming to an agreement first. The loss of love is almost inevitable when that happens.

If the dictator strategy is left unchecked, one spouse finds themselves controlled rather than a partner in a marriage. The practice of one spouse making unilateral decisions usually proves to their partner that the dictator really doesn't care about anyone but themselves.

## Dueling Dictators

I have heard many young wives complain about their husband's decisions to come and go as he pleases, make his own friends, stay out late without letting her know where he is, and other thoughtless acts, all while she is obligated to stay home in the evenings with their children, cook and clean, and make herself available to him for sex whenever needed.

At first, they try to adjust to living with their new husbands by accommodating his wishes. But before long they begin to realize that what they're experiencing is nothing more than old-fashioned selfishness. He's expecting her to take care of things without considering her feelings. As resentment grows, the subordinate spouse decides to stage a coup, raising themselves to dictator status. They fight back by creating the **dueling dictators strategy**.

Now that she's on equal footing, she objects to his plans when they are not in her interest. But she goes one step further. As a new dictator, she makes plans for him that are not in his interest and tells him what to do. What happens next is all-out war, with each side trying to impose their will and control the other. After each argument, the stronger and more determined spouse wins the decision, which means that his or her solution is put into effect. But the losing dictator is already plotting more carefully for the next battle.

Unfortunately, millions of unhappy couples use the dueling dictators strategy to try to resolve their conflicts. It makes problem-solving unpleasant for all involved, but at least it seems fairer than the dictator strategy. After all, no one loses all the time with this strategy. Now, instead of one spouse being victimized, both spouses are victimized!

## Anarchy

Dueling dictators are so miserable that they often feel as if they have only two choices. They can either divorce or create a marriage where they stay out of each other's way. To continue in misery is simply not an option.

So those who choose to remain married begin to use what I call the **anarchy strategy**. This strategy gives up hope of resolving conflict with agreement and takes the position, "every man for himself!" A husband, wife, or sometimes both, just do whatever they want and ignore each other's feelings and interests. Anarchy is their last resort. But just like governments in anarchy, anarchic marriages become chaotic and soon fall apart. Ultimately, these marriages are not really marriages at all.

A few years ago, as I was thumbing through an issue of *Reader's Digest*, I came upon an article entitled, "The Science of a Happy Marriage" by Michael Gurian.* The subtitle of the article was particularly intriguing: "By nature, men and women aren't made for each other. How to outsmart our DNA and live happily ever after."

The thesis of this article was that couples experience five stages in marriage. They are (1) romance, (2) disillusionment, (3) power struggle, (4) awakening, and (5) long-term marriage. We all understand the romance, disillusionment, and power struggle stages, but what does Gurian mean by "awakening" and "long-term marriage"? Awakening, according to Gurian, is coming to the awareness that romance is possible only in the beginning of a relationship. So if a couple wants a long-term marriage they must give up hope for a romantic marriage. When that happens, according to Gurian and others (such as the writings of Locke Rush), the couple is able to settle into the only long-term relationship that can work for a husband and wife.

*Michael Gurian, "The Science of a Happy Marriage," *Reader's Digest*, August 2004, 151–55.

But that relationship resembles what I've called anarchy—each spouse going his and her own way. Gurian claims that they should have different sets of friends, create separate hobbies, go on separate vacations, and in general create totally different lifestyles. They experience a realization that they can remain married only if they have as little to do with each other as possible. After going through an irrational struggle to blend their lives, something that's required in a romantic relationship, they finally realize that living independent lives is the only way for their marriage to survive.

Anarchy is their ultimate solution to marital problem-solving.

Really? Is that what every couple must look forward to in life? Is that how you want your marriage to end?

Anarchy only makes sense when the dueling dictators strategy is the only other alternative. The disillusionment and power struggles faced by a couple who fights over every conflict make anarchy seem reasonable.

## Democracy

But there is another way for a couple to resolve conflict—a way that maintains their romantic relationship. It's the **democracy strategy**, where a husband and wife don't make a decision until they're both in agreement. The democracy strategy for marital conflict requires unanimous consent. Neither spouse can impose their will on the other.

Gurian and others feel that men and women are so different that mutual agreement is a goal that's totally unrealistic. And maybe the experience you've had so far in your marriage leads you to feel the same way. But my own marital experience and the experience of millions of other couples who have learned to negotiate the right way are proof that marital problems can be resolved democratically. When that happens, the romance stage of marriage persists indefinitely.

In my example of the exhausted wife and the television-watching husband, there are a host of decisions that need to be made about what they do between four o'clock in the afternoon and seven o'clock in the evening. Clearly, they have not made those decisions jointly with a win-win outcome. And as a result, both the husband and the wife are making Love Bank withdrawals. The husband is making withdrawals from the wife's Love Bank because of his habit of watching TV when he comes home each evening. But the wife is also making withdrawals from the husband's Love Bank by being so demanding whenever she comes home to face all the extra work. She's certainly no treat to be around at the end of the day.

The point I want to make as clearly as possible is that while this couple need to change what they do after work, demands will not lead to a mutually satisfying solution. They lead to a solution where one person tries to gain at the other's expense. From the wife's perspective, turning the TV off and getting the husband to help a little is a fair solution to the problem. But the husband doesn't see things the same way. In fact, the husband regards his wife's demands as abusive and controlling. In the actual case from which I took this example, he left the house and went back to work, with his wife in tears as he left.

After counseling thousands of couples, I don't know of a single example where demands have created the ultimate solution to a problem. Instead of leading to a solution, demands lead to resentment, and in some cases a spouse may develop an extremely negative emotional reaction to the very thought of it. Psychologists call it an *aversive reaction*. It often takes the form of a very sick feeling in the pit of the stomach whenever there are thoughts about having to do something that's been associated with pain or suffering.

That's what happened to Karen when she tried to meet Jim's demand for sex. She developed an aversion to sex, and eventually they didn't have any sex at all. Karen was not only resentful that Jim would force her to have sex with him, but she also developed an emotional reaction to sex that made it an absolute nightmare for her. Her husband's demand for sex ultimately made it **less** likely that she would meet his sexual need.

So even when a demand seems to work in the short run and you get your way, it usually makes it more difficult for you to get your way in the long run. If you need something from each other, the worst thing you can do is to demand it, because demands make your spouse less likely to do it for you in the future.

I want to help both of you get what you need from each other in your marriage and I want you to be in love with each other. But you'll fail to do either of these things if you're in the habit of making demands. You won't have your needs met and you won't be in love. You should have zero tolerance for selfish demands in your marriage.

*Unlike all the other strategies we've seen, the democracy strategy addresses conflicts and resolves them with no victims.*

Unlike all the other strategies we've seen, the democracy strategy addresses conflicts and resolves them with no victims. The outcome of every decision is in the best interest of both spouses.

So why isn't the democracy strategy used in all, or even most, marriages? It's because we are not born with an instinct for democracy. Instead, we're born with an instinct to get our way at any cost. That attitude puts the dictatorship strategy into play soon after marriage begins. And once that happens, the dueling dictators and anarchy strategies are often not far behind.

So the democracy strategy will not seem as natural to you as the others—it requires time and thought. But it's the only sensible way for you to make marital decisions. It not only provides wise solutions to your problems, but it will also draw you much closer to each other emotionally. And that's a basic requirement for every romantic relationship.

In the next chapter, I offer you a plan to help you overcome the habit of making selfish demands, and to create the habit of making thoughtful requests. The change will not only revolutionize your ability to resolve conflicts once and for all, but it will also help you restore your love for each other.

I'll also introduce a new rule to you that makes the democracy strategy possible. It will force you to find a mutually acceptable solution before any action is taken. It's called the **Policy of Joint Agreement**: *Never do anything without an enthusiastic agreement between you and your spouse.*

# —— Key Principles ——

If you command your spouse to do something for you that benefits you at your spouse's expense, you are guilty of making a **selfish demand**.

Selfish demands are abusive and controlling, but they seem reasonable to make when spouses are frustrated. Abuse in marriage is the *deliberate attempt of a spouse to cause the other to be unhappy*. So demands are a form of verbal abuse because they certainly do cause unhappiness and they are done with intent. Demands are also controlling because they are made with the purpose of forcing a spouse to do something against their will.

The most common win-lose way that couples try to resolve conflicts begins with the **sacrifice strategy** where each spouse gives to the other spouse whatever they want without revealing that they are losing so that the other can win. This is usually followed by the **capitulation strategy** where they willingly give each other whatever is desired, but reveal their loss. The **dictatorship strategy** is next in line, where one spouse tries to tell the other spouse how conflicts will be resolved. Selfish demands are used to try to resolve a problem. But it doesn't take long before the other spouse changes it into the **dueling dictators strategy**, where both spouses fight for control. Now they are making demands of each other. Finally, when couples can no longer tolerate the fighting but want to remain married, they use the **anarchy strategy**. This form of conflict resolution assumes that most marital conflicts cannot be resolved to benefit both spouses. There are no demands because spouses make their decisions independently of each other.

The **democracy strategy** is a win-win approach to resolving conflicts. Its goal is to resolve all conflicts in a way that both spouses are winners.

You should have zero tolerance for selfish demands in your marriage.

# Consider This . . . ────────────

1. Are selfish demands a problem in your marriage? To answer that question, complete the selfish demands page (page 212) of the Love Busters Questionnaire in Appendix B. Make two enlarged copies, one for each of you, so that you will have enough space to write your answers.

2. Were you able to identify selfish demands in your marriage? When one of you makes a selfish demand does the other spouse bring it to his or her attention? What have the consequences of such feedback been? Do you tend to punish each other for complaining about demands, or do you appreciate the feedback? From now on, are you willing to have zero tolerance for selfish demands?

3. The six strategies for marital conflict resolution are sacrifice, capitulation, dictatorship, dueling dictators, anarchy, and democracy. Which of these strategies do you use most of the time when you face a conflict? How do you feel about trying to use the democracy strategy for a while? In the next chapter, I'll show you how it's done.

# 5

Selfish Demands: *Part 2*

## How to Turn Selfish Demands into Thoughtful Requests

Democracy isn't easy. And neither is the democracy strategy in marriage. But for civilization and marriage alike, the rewards found in solutions that blend the interests of others are well worth the added effort. So what's the best way to actually go about reaching an enthusiastic agreement when you and your spouse want something from each other?

Returning to the example of the harried wife and well-rested, TV-watching husband that I used in the last chapter, most would agree that it's unfair for her to do all the work. But trying to force him to help doesn't turn out very well in marriage. He feels resentful at being told what to do, and even if he ends up helping tonight, tomorrow brings the same battle. What a couple needs is a permanent solution that both spouses enthusiastically support.

That's the goal of the democracy strategy—to be guided by a new rule that you will live by for the rest of your lives together. I call that rule the **Policy of Joint Agreement:** *Never do anything without an enthusiastic agreement between you and your spouse.*

This policy encourages you to approach your spouse for help in a way that will lead to an enthusiastic agreement.

But why have an enthusiastic agreement? Wouldn't a reluctant agreement be enough? To answer those questions, let's revisit what it takes to make Love Bank deposits. An enthusiastic agreement means that you are making deposits into both of your Love Banks simultaneously—a win-win outcome. A reluctant agreement, while often seen as at least better than no agreement at all, leads to deposits into only one spouse's Love Bank. So if you want to be in love with each other, I strongly encourage you to get into the habit of reaching enthusiastic agreements.

> **The Policy of Joint Agreement**
>
> *Never do anything without an enthusiastic agreement between you and your spouse.*

Obviously, the selfish demand, *do this for me or else,* cannot possibly lead to an enthusiastic agreement and is always a violation of the Policy of Joint Agreement. But what about the request, *would you please help me with this?* While you are not threatening your spouse when you make that request, it still doesn't satisfy the conditions of the Policy of Joint Agreement. You must go one step further. You must ask your spouse how he or she *feels* about helping you. The answer to that question will tell you whether or not you have an enthusiastic agreement.

So whenever you want something from each other, I recommend the **thoughtful request,** *How would you feel about doing this for me?* It's thoughtful because you are asking your spouse to reveal his or her feelings and interests, and it's a request because you are not commanding your spouse to do something for you. But even if your thoughtful request is denied in its present form, your thoughtfulness opens the door to further discussion. Conditions that might lead to an enthusiastic agreement can be pursued.

*How would you feel about doing this for me?* is a question that reflects your care for each other. And it makes an enthusiastic willingness to provide that care far more likely than a demand, or even a simple request, ever could.

If your thoughtful request results in a negative response, the Policy of Joint Agreement offers you two choices: Either abandon the request or try to discover ways to make it possible—with your spouse's enthusiastic agreement. That's where negotiation begins.

But maybe you're so accustomed to making selfish demands (or sacrificing and capitulating) that you've never really developed much skill negotiating. In fact, you may think that it's impossible to reach enthusiastic agreements in your marriage because you are both so stubborn and stuck in your ways of doing things. My response to you is that there's no time like the present to develop the skill you need to break through the barriers that have prevented you from finding win-win ways to help each other. It's simply a matter of practicing a time-honored method of negotiation until it's become a habit to both of you.

What is this time-honored method that is well known in business transactions, but usually ignored in marriage? I call it the **Four Guidelines for Successful Negotiation in Marriage**. The Policy of Joint Agreement opens the door to the possibility of negotiating, and the Four Guidelines for Successful Negotiation in Marriage lead you to an enthusiastic agreement.

### The Four Guidelines for Successful Negotiation in Marriage

#### *Guideline 1: Set ground rules to make your negotiation pleasant and safe.*

Most couples view marital negotiation as a trip to the torture chamber. That's because their efforts are usually fruitless, and they come away from the experience battered and bruised. Who wants to negotiate when you have nothing but disappointment and pain to look forward to?

So before you begin to negotiate, set some basic ground rules to make sure that you both enjoy the experience. Since you should negotiate as often as conflict arises, you'll not hesitate to address the issue if you know it will be enjoyable and safe. I suggest three basic ground rules:

**Ground Rule 1:** *Try to be pleasant and cheerful throughout negotiations*. It's fairly easy to start discussing an issue while in a good mood. But negotiations can open a can of worms and create negative emotional reactions. Your spouse may begin to feel uncomfortable about something you say.

I know how upset and defensive couples can become when they first tell each other how they feel. So I tell them what I'm telling you—try to be as positive and cheerful as you can be, especially if your spouse says something that offends you. If you can't do it, postpone the discussion.

**Ground Rule 2:** *Put safety first—do not make demands, show disrespect, or become angry when you negotiate, even if your spouse does.* Once the cat is out of the bag and you've told your spouse what you'd like him or her to do for you, and you've asked how he or she would feel about doing it for you, you've entered one of the most dangerous phases of negotiation. Your spouse may not be enthusiastic about helping you in the way you have proposed, and that may hurt your feelings. When that happens, you may be tempted to retaliate. Unless you make a special effort to resist attacking your reluctant spouse with disrespect and anger, and turning your thoughtful request into a selfish demand, you will be reverting to the dictator strategy and your negotiation will turn into an argument. But if you can keep each other safe, you'll be able to use your intelligence to get the help you need.

**Ground Rule 3:** *If you reach an impasse where you do not seem to be getting anywhere, or if one of you is starting to make demands, show disrespect, or become angry, stop negotiating and come back to the issue later.* Just because you can't resolve a problem at a particular point in time doesn't mean you can't find an intelligent solution in the future. Don't let an impasse prevent you from giving yourself a chance to think about the issue. Let it incubate for a while, and you'll be amazed what your mind can do.

### Guideline 2: Identify the problem from both perspectives.

Once you've set ground rules that guarantee a safe and enjoyable discussion, you're ready to negotiate. But where do you begin? First, you must state the problem and then try to understand it from the perspectives of both you and your spouse.

Most couples go into marital negotiation without doing their homework. They don't fully understand the problem itself, nor do they understand each other's perspectives. In many cases, they are not even sure what they really want.

What is it that you want from your spouse and why do you want it? Why would your spouse feel reluctant to fulfill your request? Respect is the key to success in this phase of negotiation. Once the problem has been identified and you hear each other's perspectives, it's extremely important to try to understand each other instead of trying to straighten each other out. Remember that your goal is enthusiastic agreement, and that can't happen if you reject each other's perspectives as being unreasonable. The only way you'll reach an enthusiastic agreement is to come up with a solution that accommodates both perspectives as they are presented.

This point is so important that I will repeat it. **You will not solve your problem if you are disrespectful of each other's perspectives.** In this second stage of negotiation, you are simply to gather information that will help you understand what it will take to solve your problem. If you reject your spouse's opinions, you will be ignoring the facts. You should not talk over your spouse, try to talk your spouse out of his or her opinion, or even use mannerisms that could be interpreted as disrespectful.

### *Guideline 3: Brainstorm with abandon.*

You've set the ground rules. You've identified the problem and discovered each other's perspectives. Now you're ready for the creative part—looking for a way to get the help you need with your spouse's enthusiastic agreement. I know that can seem impossible if you and your spouse have been in the habit of giving in to each other when demands have been made. But if you put your minds to it, you'll think of options that please you both.

You won't get very far if you allow yourself to think, "If she really loves me, she'll let me do this," or "He'll do this for me, if he cares about me." Care in marriage is not sacrificial care—it's **mutual** care. That means both spouses should want the other to be happy, and neither spouse should want the other to be unhappy. If you care about your spouse, you should never expect, or even accept, your spouse's sacrifice as a solution to a problem unless you are facing an emergency that threatens your health or safety.

Granted, mutual sacrifice can be made with mutual enthusiasm. We have all learned to postpone gratification to achieve a goal. So if you and your spouse both agree to make personal sacrifices for mutually held objectives, there won't be any love lost. A spouse working to support the other spouse's education is an example of personal sacrifice being used to achieve a joint objective. It's made with mutual enthusiastic agreement.

But I warn you to avoid the "I'll do what you want me to do this time if you do what I want you to do next time" solution. This isn't a win-win solution: One of you ends up unhappy whenever the other is happy. And if you've ever used this strategy, you may have noticed that your spouse doesn't always follow through with his or her end of the bargain.

Win-lose solutions are common in marriage because most couples don't understand how to arrive at win-win solutions. Their concept of fairness is that both spouses should suffer equally. But isn't it better to find solutions where neither spouse suffers? With a little creativity and practice, you can find solutions that make both of you happy.

With sacrifice and capitulation out of the question, you're ready to brainstorm. And at first, quantity is often more important than quality. So let your minds run wild; go with any thought that might satisfy both of you simultaneously. The best and most creative solutions often take time to discover, so carry something with you that allows you to jot down ideas as they come to you. When you let your creative juices flow, you are more likely to find a lasting solution.

### Guideline 4: Choose the solution that meets the conditions of the Policy of Joint Agreement—mutual and enthusiastic agreement.

After brainstorming, you'll have both good and bad solutions. Good solutions are those both you and your spouse consider desirable. Bad solutions, on the other hand, take the feelings of one spouse into account at the expense of the other. The best solution is the one that makes you and your spouse most enthusiastic.

Many problems are relatively easy to solve if you know you must take each other's feelings into account. That's because you become aware of what it will take to reach a mutual agreement. Instead of considering options that clearly are not in your spouse's best interest, you think of options that would make both you and your spouse happy.

A habit is formed by repeating a particular behavior. So if you want your spouse to be consistent in helping you with the problem you face, the help you need should be repeated until it becomes a habit.

To illustrate this point, let's take a closer look at the exhausted wife's dilemma. If she only expects to get the help she needs when she's exhausted, it's not likely that her husband will create the habit of helping her at times of greatest need. She will be forced to reintroduce her need every time she feels exhausted, along with a new session of negotiation.

But if she and her husband can conclude their negotiation with a plan to create the habit of doing the dishes together every night in a way that would be enjoyable for both of them, when Tuesday night rolls around and she's exhausted, his help is a done deal. She gets what she needs because it's something they've already negotiated with each other and they're doing it in a way that makes deposits into both of their Love Banks. By forming a new habit, the issue doesn't need to be reintroduced through negotiation.

The husband who's sitting there watching television while his exhausted wife slaves away at the dishes isn't a lazy husband. He's a husband who is in the habit of watching television after dinner. This man could just as easily be in the habit of helping his wife with the dishes and enjoying it just as much as watching television. The problem is, since he's already in the habit of watching television, he's going to be very upset with a wife who simply turns the television off and demands that he start washing the dishes. That isn't the way to get the job done. It creates anger and resentment and you lose a lot of love units while those dishes are being dried.

But if she explains her need in a thoughtful way and they get into the right habits, the evening that this husband and wife spend together with their children can become predictably enjoyable. That's because they've designed it to be enjoyable for each other. They've thought it through and decided to do things for each other that they find enjoyable. And that enjoyable routine is repeated night after night.

If you follow the four guidelines I've suggested, negotiation can be an important way to learn about each other. And when you reach a solution that makes you both happy, you'll make substantial deposits into each other's Love Banks. In the end, the Policy of Joint Agreement not only helps you become a great negotiator, it also protects your love for each other.

But as you've read my guidelines for successful negotiation, you may wonder if you have what it takes to build a lifetime of love. The process of negotiation that I've described may seem contrived—just not the way normal people do things. All those steps, and all that discussion: it's just too much work. But as I explain throughout this book, habits make life a lot easier, and you can get into the habit of becoming expert negotiators. Besides, what is the alternative? Failing to get what you need from each other because you just don't know how to do it.

Which would you prefer? Resolving your conflict once and for all without ever having to deal with it again, or having an argument every time the conflict arises without resolving it? Knowing how to resolve marital conflicts the right way is one of the most important skill sets that you can ever learn. It's the smart thing to do in marriage.

With practice, any couple can do it. And once you establish the habit of negotiating with each other, it will be easy to run through the steps whenever there is a problem to solve. It's like learning to type, or playing the piano. At first it seems awkward, but with practice, it seems almost instinctive.

If you and your spouse have found yourselves acting more like dictators than sweethearts, it may sound overwhelming to switch to successful negotiations. But the guidelines can be implemented almost effortlessly if you practice them. Any behavior can seem automatic when repeated often enough.

Your spouse probably wants to help you—even when he or she initially refuses your request. It isn't the helping that's being refused—it's the form the help takes. If the requested task is unpleasant, there may be another way to get the job done that is enjoyable.

Mutually enthusiastic agreements are not only a good way to get what you need in marriage, they are also the only way that is not controlling and abusive. If you want consistent help from each other, there is no better way to get it than through an enthusiastic agreement.

## Replacing the Habit of Selfish Demands with the Habit of Thoughtful Requests

Are you both willing to eliminate selfish demands and replace them with thoughtful requests? If so, you will be embarking on a very important path that will make your marriage much more fulfilling. But it's a difficult path to take. The reason that it's so difficult is that habits are hard to break, and selfish demands are no exception.

At first you might think that it can't be that difficult to make a change from *get up and help me with the children,* to *how would you feel about helping me with the children?* Aside from the gnawing feeling at first that it just doesn't seem right to use those words, what could be so hard about changing the way you ask for help?

But it isn't just the words. It's also the intent. When you make a demand, you give your spouse no right to refuse. Or at least, if your spouse refuses, there will be consequences that you will happily impose. Requests, on the other hand, give your spouse the right to refuse without consequences. But a thoughtful request goes one step further. It asks for your spouse's enthusiastic help. It wants help in a way that your spouse will enjoy. If there is reluctance, the Policy of Joint Agreement and Four Guidelines for Successful Negotiation in Marriage should kick in to get the help you need with enthusiastic agreement.

*It boils down to this: spouses should never try to force each other to do their bidding.*

It boils down to this: spouses should never try to force each other to do their bidding. As complicated as it may sound to you to resolve your conflicts through thoughtful negotiation, it's the only reasonable way to make sure that you are making deposits into both of your Love Banks simultaneously.

## The Selfish Demands Worksheet and the Thoughtful Requests Worksheet

The best ways to measure your success in overcoming selfish demands and replacing them with thoughtful requests is to record all instances of both. So you will need two worksheets for those records: title one "Selfish Demands Worksheet," and the other, "Thoughtful Requests Worksheet."

The Selfish Demands Worksheet should list each selfish demand by the day, date, and time that it was made, with a brief description of what was said and the circumstances surrounding it. The Thoughtful Requests Worksheet should record the same information when thoughtful requests are made.

The spouse who is the recipient of selfish demands is to complete both worksheets, and is the final judge as to what is and what is not a selfish demand and thoughtful request. If you are both trying to replace selfish demands with thoughtful requests, each of you should complete both worksheets.

The goal is to completely eliminate any instance of a selfish demand, and to fill the Thoughtful Requests Worksheet each week. When you and your spouse are both satisfied that the habit of making selfish demands has been replaced with the habit of making thoughtful requests, you will no longer need to use these worksheets. But because habits are hard to break, plan on keeping these records for at least three months.

Let each other know if you find yourselves drifting from thoughtful requests back to selfish demands. And try not to react defensively when your spouse gives you such feedback. You may be surprised the first time your spouse reminds you that you are making a selfish demand. From your perspective, you were making a request, not a demand. But if you have been in the habit of making demands in the past, you're likely to revert back to making them without even consciously realizing it. And only your spouse will be able to recognize the difference between a selfish demand that's disguised as a thoughtful request, and a genuine thoughtful request. Until your spouse starts interpreting what you ask as requests, you'll need to work on not only your intent, but also your phrasing.

Don't make the mistake that many couples make where you begin arguing about whether something was or wasn't a selfish demand. As far as I'm concerned, whoever is making the request must convince the other spouse that it's not a demand. If the spouse receiving the request is completely honest, you'll learn quite a bit about how to adjust to his or her feelings. By doing that, you'll be in a great position to create a lifestyle that's full of passion for both of you.

How comfortable are you in making thoughtful requests of each other? When spouses are in the habit of making selfish demands, they are often reluctant to make as many requests of each other as they should. They tend to use demands as a last resort to getting what they think they deserve, and forget about asking for what they need from each other. By learning how to make thoughtful requests, you will probably ask for more from each other, and receive more, than you did when you made demands.

> *Demands may get the job done in the present, but they sabotage the future.*

Your effort to convert selfish demands into thoughtful requests is a great way to effectively communicate what you need. As you both learn to accommodate each other's needs in ways that are enjoyable to both of you, you will eventually be in the habit of getting what you need most from each other voluntarily, instead of trying to do it in ways that are controlling and abusive. Ultimately you want to receive help without even having to ask. In other words, you want your spouse to form the *habit* of helping you (as you develop the habit of helping your spouse). Demands cannot accomplish this. Demands may get the job done in the present, but they sabotage the future.

## Key Principles

If you command your spouse to do something for you that benefits you at your spouse's expense, you are guilty of making a **selfish demand**.

A **thoughtful request** is asking your spouse to do something for you, with a willingness to withdraw the request if there is reluctance and to discuss alternatives that would also be in your spouse's best interest. A thoughtful request should take the form of "How would you feel if you were to do this for me?"

The **Policy of Joint Agreement**—*never do anything without an enthusiastic agreement between you and your spouse*—helps couples avoid selfish demands by forbidding decisions that are not mutually beneficial.

The best way for couples to discover mutually beneficial solutions to problems is to follow the **Four Guidelines for Successful Negotiation in Marriage.**

Thoughtful requests will help you create habits that provide the care you need from each other. Selfish demands, on the other hand, will not lead to habits if they are granted. Instead, they may lead to aversive reactions which make it more difficult to get what you need from each other.

## Consider This . . .

1. What is the difference between a selfish demand and a thoughtful request? Have you been able to identify selfish demands in your marriage? When one of you makes a selfish demand does the other spouse bring it to his or her attention? What have the consequences of such feedback been? Do you tend to punish each other for complaining about demands, or do you appreciate the feedback?

2. What do each of you think of the Four Guidelines for Successful Negotiation in Marriage? Are you willing to practice using them to see if they work for you? Can you see how useful they would be in resolving conflicts once and for all?

3. If you feel that you need more guidance in learning how to follow the Policy of Joint Agreement and the Four Guidelines for Successful Negotiation in Marriage, I encourage you to consider following the twelve-week He Wins, She Wins Training Program. It is offered in my book *He Wins, She Wins*, and its accompanying *He Wins, She Wins Workbook*.

# 6

## Disrespectful Judgments: *Part 1*

### Who Wants to Live with a Critic?

Linda was raised by parents who worked long hours but never seemed to get ahead. Poor educational background was the main reason for their low income—neither parent graduated from high school. But their large family—five children—was also a contributing factor. Linda, her three brothers, one sister, and their parents shared a small house and just about everything else throughout her childhood.

After graduating from high school, Linda found a job as a reception-ist, which paid enough to support her. So at eighteen, she moved away from home, rented an apartment, bought her own car, and felt on top of the world.

Tom, a new executive, found Linda very attractive. At first, he just greeted her whenever he passed her desk, but the greetings turned into conversations and before long he was regularly having lunch with her. Eventually they fell in love.

Tom was well educated, having earned advanced degrees in both law and business administration. When he met Linda's family, he was im-mediately accepted and respected by them all. Her father was especially pleased that she chose to date such an intelligent man.

At first, Tom had respect for Linda and her family as well. But as their romance developed, he began making critical remarks about the decisions made by members of her family. Then, occasionally, he began to criticize Linda's decisions. Since he was so well educated, she assumed in most instances that he was correct and she was wrong. It bothered her whenever he made these critical remarks, but it happened so seldom that it did not have much effect on her love for him.

Before long they were married, and after the honeymoon Tom and Linda returned to work as husband and wife. But their relationship at work changed the very first day: Linda found herself working with her worst critic, who also happened to be her husband.

Now that they were married, Tom would bring the smallest errors to her attention and coach her on improving her posture, telephone etiquette, and other office skills. She became increasingly unhappy at work and eventually decided to quit. She used the excuse of wanting to prepare for having children, but her real reason was to escape Tom's incessant criticism. Her income, after taxes, was not enough to make much of a difference in their standard of living anyway, since Tom earned enough to support them both. Besides, she was raised to value the role of a homemaker and full-time mother.

But as soon as she quit her job, she went from the frying pan into the fire. At home Tom became even more critical than he'd been at work. He expected her to develop a high level of homemaking skills and evaluated her work each day. Her performance rarely met his standards, so she just gave up. Before long, she was spending the day watching television and sleeping.

Since his lectures on homemaking didn't seem to help, Tom turned his attention to subjects of motivation and ambition. When he came home from work, Linda had to suffer through Tom's self-improvement courses. Their discussions became so one-sided that she eventually stopped trying to explain her point of view.

Tom rationalized his efforts to straighten Linda out as his way of caring for her. He would explain that he was doing her a favor by helping her overcome weaknesses. In the end, he told Linda, she would thank him for his "coaching."

The truth was that he was being controlling and abusive. He wanted things done his way, and he didn't really care how Linda felt about it. He was trying to turn her into his personal servant. But instead of simply making demands on her, he used a more sophisticated approach to abuse—he showed disrespect in an effort to shame her into doing what he wanted. He knew that his criticism was making her unhappy, but he did nothing to protect her. His "help" was causing her to become very depressed, and his lectures made massive Love Bank withdrawals. Before long she had lost her feeling of love for him.

Linda became so depressed that Tom decided she needed professional help. First, he made an appointment to speak with me alone, to determine my competence. Then, after I passed his test, he brought her with him to the second session and wanted to be included in the interview. But I asked to speak with Linda alone while he remained in the waiting room. Within two sessions, however, I had Tom join her—for marriage counseling.

## Compassion or Abuse?

Most of us feel that our judgment is correct. When we hear others express opposing views or see them doing something differently from the way we are accustomed to doing it, we often feel that their opinions and behavior are wrong. In addition to thinking they are wrong, we might think that we need to straighten them out—for their own good. What they're doing or thinking could get them into trouble some day. So by telling them that they're wrong, and that we're right, we're actually doing them a favor. This is especially true if the person is our spouse.

Do you sometimes feel that your spouse's thinking needs to be straightened out for their own good? Do you think you're doing your spouse a big favor to lift him or her from the darkness of confusion into the light of your superior perspective? Do you think that if your spouse would only follow your advice, he or she could avoid many of life's pitfalls? If so, you're asking for trouble. You're making disrespectful judgments.

**Disrespectful judgments** are attempts to "straighten out" your spouse's attitudes, beliefs, and behavior by trying to impose your way of thinking through lecture, ridicule, threats, or other forceful means. Whenever you are being disrespectful to your spouse, you're making massive Love Bank withdrawals.

Quite frankly, we may try to convince ourselves that the true motive for our disrespectful judgments is the love and compassion we have for our spouse. But I've been convinced in my years of helping people overcome these judgments that love and compassion are not really why we're disrespectful. We're disrespectful because we are trying to get what we want from our spouse. We try to convince our spouse that we're being compassionate when we're really being abusive and controlling.

## Disrespectful Judgments—the Second Stage of Abuse and Control

When you want your spouse to do something for you, you'll be tempted to demand change. That's the first stage of abuse and control, and I explained in the last two chapters how to replace selfish demands with thoughtful requests. Thoughtful requests are more likely to motivate your spouse to make the change you need, and they also help preserve the love you have for each other.

> *Disrespectful judgments are attempts to "straighten out" your spouse's attitudes, beliefs, and behavior by trying to impose your way of thinking through lecture, ridicule, threats, or other forceful means.*

But those who have not learned that lesson, and have found that their demands are not effective, usually turn up the volume to get what they want. When demands don't work, disrespectful judgments are not far behind. It's a more sophisticated form of control, because it *seems* to be motivated by care rather than selfishness. When making disrespectful judgments, you try to fool your spouse into thinking that you're being thoughtful.

If Tom had understood his true motives for trying to straighten out Linda, he would have known that he was trying to get his way at her expense. He wanted her to do things his way at work, and then when she quit, he wanted her to do things his way at home. The ruse of care was used to hide his controlling and abusive ways. Linda knew that whatever he was doing hurt her terribly, but she was duped into thinking it was somehow good for her.

Many spouses will see through this deception, and when their spouse makes disrespectful judgments they know it's based on selfishness. For them, the Love Buster is exposed for what it is. But even if, like Linda, a spouse *is* deceived into thinking that disrespect is motivated by care, the result is the same—it destroys the feeling of love. That's because disrespect always hurts. Even though Linda believed that Tom was doing the right thing by trying to straighten her out, his disrespectful judgments still destroyed her love for him.

## Ridicule Hurts, Too

Tom's efforts to straighten Linda out were not her only problem. Whenever she expressed an opinion, Tom tended to make fun of her. He thought her ideas were so stupid that they were funny, and told her so whenever she tried to express herself.

While disrespectful judgments are usually an effort to try to make your spouse do what you want, sometimes in marriage the sole purpose of disrespect is entertainment. For some, whenever they ridicule their spouse, they're not trying to change his or her behavior, but rather, they're using the situation as something to laugh at—something that they find amusing.

When it comes right down to it, almost all humor is ridicule of one form or another. Most jokes are designed to point out the foolishness of people's thinking or behavior. But in marriage, making your spouse the butt of ridicule is extremely dangerous. Not only is it very hurtful to the one being ridiculed, but if you're not careful, the tables can be turned and the ridiculed spouse can return ridicule in a way that doubles the pain. Some spouses raise ridicule to an art form where they use every opportunity to make fun of each other. But it's not fun for the person being ridiculed. In fact, it usually makes huge Love Bank withdrawals.

In marriage you have an opportunity to know each other's deepest secrets and greatest weaknesses. You know some of each other's most embarrassing moments, which leave both of you very vulnerable to each other's ridicule. It's extremely important for you to know each other so well that you thoroughly understand your weaknesses. But that creates a vulnerability and responsibility that's almost unprecedented in life. The price of learning each other's deepest secrets should be a guarantee never to use that information to hurt or try to make fun of each other.

*Disrespectful judgments are an instinctive way to make your spouse feel miserable.*

Disrespectful judgments are an instinctive way to make your spouse feel miserable. Since you make Love Bank withdrawals whenever you offend your spouse, disrespect is a real Love Buster.

## Disrespect Is the Opposite of Admiration

Admiration is one of the ten most important emotional needs in marriage that I identify in the companion to this book, *His Needs, Her Needs*. It's of vital importance in marriage to be an admiring spouse because it makes such large Love Bank deposits. We should be the president of our spouse's fan club if we want our spouse to be in love with us.

But disrespectful judgments turn what should be an admiring spouse into a spouse's worst critic. Instead of making huge Love Bank deposits, huge withdrawals are made. And the more a spouse needs admiration, the more disrespectful judgments hurt.

*But what if I really don't respect my spouse? What if there's nothing to admire? Isn't it being dishonest to pretend showing respect, when I am actually critical of what my spouse is thinking or doing?*

The answer to that very important question will be addressed more completely in the upcoming chapters on dishonesty, chapters 10 and 11. But for now let me make the point that if you don't like something that your spouse is thinking or doing, being disrespectful isn't the way to motivate change. It makes your spouse *less likely* to change.

I'm not suggesting that you express admiration for something that you don't admire. But I am advising you in the strongest way possible to avoid expressing disrespect when your spouse does something that bothers you. It's one thing to say that something your spouse is thinking or doing makes you unhappy, but it's quite another to say that it's wrong. One is a complaint that is perfectly legitimate in marriage while the other is a criticism that will drive a wedge between you and your spouse.

## Disrespectful Judgments Don't Get the Job Done

Tom preferred using demands to get his way with Linda because it's the simplest way to try to control a spouse. But he found that after a while she resisted his demands. When he told her that she was not cleaning their house to his standards, she would sometimes argue back that if he didn't like the way the house looked, he could try cleaning it himself for a while.

So Tom's demands had to be reinforced. He would explain that if she didn't keep the house clean to his standards, she was shirking her responsibility as a wife. In other words, he tried to make her feel guilty about the way she performed her housekeeping duties.

Since this approach to marital problem-solving is so common, and so instinctive, I want you to clearly recognize this fact: While your disrespectful judgments may seem sensible to you at the time, they hurt your spouse. And because they hurt, they're abusive.

But they're not only abusive, they're also ineffective. They don't get the job done long term. At first, Linda tried a little harder to meet Tom's housekeeping standards, but she eventually gave up almost entirely. She didn't keep the house cleaner after Tom scolded her—she simply became depressed.

And yet, even though disrespectful judgments don't get the job done, it's what every couple usually does when they have a fight. They make demands, and then back up the demands with disrespectful judgments. It's so instinctive that it may be difficult for you to understand the point I'm trying to make. But just think about your own fights for a moment. Have you been disrespectful to each other? Has it gotten you anywhere? Are you happier after you rake each other over the coals?

And that's the point. Disrespectful judgments are abusive because they cause unhappiness, they are controlling because they try to force your spouse into your way of thinking, and they're ineffective. They just don't work.

You should have zero tolerance for disrespectful judgments.

## The Road to Recovery

When Linda became depressed, Tom assumed that she had not learned the lessons he tried to teach her, so he pressed on with even greater diligence. But the harder he pressed, the more depressed she became. He was so convinced he was right that he was oblivious to both the pain he was inflicting on her and the failure of his method.

The first time I spoke with Linda, she explained how unpleasant her life had become since she married Tom. She used to enjoy housework, and looked forward to raising children. But now that Tom expected her to become a professional home economist, a whole lifetime of failure loomed before her. Raising children no longer appealed to her, because it would only increase the ways that Tom could criticize her. She felt useless and trapped. And if that wasn't bad enough, her sexual attraction to Tom had disappeared entirely. Everything he expected of her, including lovemaking, had become repulsive.

In my session with Tom, I explained to him that, in his effort to help his wife, he'd overlooked her emotional reactions. Perhaps there was some value in his goals for her—we all want to improve—but his failure to consider her feelings made his advice useless. Instead of encouraging change, he caused her to become depressed.

Since Tom really did care a great deal for Linda and wanted her to be healthy and happy, he was willing to test my theory. If she recovered from her depression, he was willing to make the changes permanent. By this time, he was looking for a new approach, because her depression was making him unhappy. Anything he could do to make her more cheerful would also be in his best interest.

I focused attention on the way Tom and Linda made decisions. Until they came to my office, Tom tried to make many of Linda's decisions for her. And he rarely consulted her about her feelings on those issues. Linda had very little confidence in her own judgment, and the longer she'd been married, the more convinced she became that Tom was smarter. So she let him make decisions for her.

But even if he were smarter, he was in no position to make decisions for her if her feelings and interests were not considered. And even then, if their problems were to be solved the right way, he should make all of his decisions with her active participation. They should make decisions together.

The more you understand your spouse's feelings and interests, the more you'll understand and appreciate why your spouse thinks and behaves the way he or she does. And the less likely it is that you'll be disrespectful in your efforts to change those attitudes and behaviors.

If you show respect for your spouse's opinions and ways of doing things, you are in a position to motivate change. But the change must be seen as beneficial to your spouse. And it must be with your spouse's enthusiastic agreement. Sound familiar? It's the Policy of Joint Agreement.

In marriage, a husband and wife's differing perspectives and value systems can bring benefit to both. Each partner brings both wisdom and foolishness to the marriage. By respectfully discussing each person's beliefs and values, the couple has an opportunity to create a superior system. But the task must be approached with mutual respect if it is to work. Without that respect, the husband and wife cannot improve their values and behavior—and they will lose their love for each other.

## Using the Policy of Joint Agreement to Create Change

If Tom was to overcome disrespectful judgments, Linda had to become an equal partner in their decision-making. He needed to understand and respect her perspective on each issue they faced, and give her equal power in coming to final decisions. They needed the democracy strategy in resolving their conflicts. So I offered Tom a plan that would help him respect Linda's opinions.

The plan began with the Policy of Joint Agreement: *Never do anything without an enthusiastic agreement between you and your spouse.*

This rule gave Tom and Linda a new perspective on their goal for making decisions. From then on, Tom could never force his way of thinking on her, because that would not result in her enthusiastic agreement. He could not shame her; he could not talk over her; he could not ridicule her. Those tactics might lead to a reluctant agreement, but not to an enthusiastic agreement. If he wanted her to change her mind or behavior, he had to do it with profound respect for her.

After Tom and Linda agreed to follow the Policy of Joint Agreement, we focused attention on the details of their joint decision-making as I described in the last chapter. To get an enthusiastic agreement with Linda, Tom had to learn to treat her opinions and behavior with respect. At the same time, Linda needed help in developing a higher regard for her own perspective and feelings.

The goals of marital negotiation should be: (1) to avoid making Love Bank withdrawals, and (2) to resolve conflicts—in that order. That way you will have many opportunities to resolve conflict because the process will always be painless. But as soon as you do anything while you negotiate that your spouse finds unpleasant, it's no longer effective negotiation, and your opportunities to negotiate are likely to dwindle. The entire process must be safe and enjoyable or your spouse will try to avoid it entirely.

If you feel you must force your spouse to do or think what you want at all costs, the cost will be love units, and you will also be unsuccessful. But even if you were able to force your spouse to do what you want for a while, you can't force your spouse to love you. Only a process of negotiation that leads you to enthusiastic agreements can achieve that objective.

## Key Principles

**Disrespectful judgments** are attempts to "straighten out" your spouse's attitudes, beliefs, and behavior by trying to impose your way of thinking through lecture, ridicule, threats, or other forceful means.

When selfish demands fail to get what a spouse needs from the other, the next instinctive approach tends to use disrespectful judgments.

Disrespectful judgments are abusive and controlling, but they're often disguised as a way to care for your spouse.

Effective negotiation requires respect for your spouse's opposing opinion.

Failure to reach agreement on attitudes and beliefs will not destroy your love for each other, as long as you follow the Policy of Joint Agreement whenever you make decisions. But being disrespectful about your differing views will not only fail to change those views, it may also destroy your love for each other.

You should have zero tolerance for disrespectful judgments.

## Consider This . . .

1. Are disrespectful judgments a problem in your marriage? To answer that question, complete the disrespectful judgments page (page 213) of the Love Busters Questionnaire in Appendix B. Make two enlarged copies, one for each of you, so that you will have enough space to write your answers.

2. Were you able to identify disrespectful judgments in your marriage? When one spouse makes a disrespectful judgment does the other spouse bring it to his or her attention? What have the consequences of such feedback been? Do you tend to punish each other for complaining about disrespect, or do you appreciate the feedback?

3. Review the Policy of Joint Agreement again with each other. What is it? Why is it important for you to make decisions that take each other's feelings into account? Why is an enthusiastic agreement important?

# 7

## Disrespectful Judgments: *Part 2*

### How to Turn Disrespectful Judgments into Respectful Persuasion

Put yourself on the receiving end of disrespectful judgments. Few conversations are more infuriating than those in which someone tries to tell you that they're right and you're wrong. And then to prove you're wrong, they belittle your opinion and try to force you to accept their opinion. Those who badger you rarely, if ever, convert you to their way of thinking. You end up wanting to end all contact with them.

On the other hand, when someone makes an effort to consider your opinion before presenting their own, you're far more open to an alternative view.

One of a salesperson's first lessons is to understand the need of the prospective buyer before presenting a product. The prospective buyer will consider the product if it meets a need, *but if he or she doesn't need it*, the salesperson wastes everybody's time.

Have you ever been called on the telephone (in the evening) by a telemarketing salesperson who wants to sell you a new telephone service? "I'm satisfied with my existing service," you may answer, trying to explain that you have no need for change. But instead of politely ending the conversation, the telemarketer begins to read the sales pitch as if you had not spoken. I react to such an approach by mentally labeling that company as one I will never do business with, even if they offer me *free* telephone service!

Linda and Tom, the couple I referenced in the last chapter, are a good example of how disrespectful judgments fail to achieve a productive outcome and destroy romantic love all at the same time. It doesn't make any sense for couples to use disrespectful judgments for any reason. But if they're using them to try to change each other's minds, it's about the worst way to do it.

## The Value of Expressing Emotional Reactions

Linda's primary weakness was her very low opinion of her judgment. Tom's primary weakness was his very high opinion of his judgment. So high, in fact, that he didn't think he needed to seriously consider Linda's perspective at all. She needed to become more assertive in expressing herself to him, and he had to learn to value her perspective.

To help Linda express herself more assertively, I taught her to explain her opinions in emotional as well as propositional terms. In other words, in addition to describing her assumptions, she could defend her position by simply explaining that it made her feel comfortable to think the way she did. She could also explain that alternative ways of thinking made her feel uncomfortable. She did not need to explain why she felt that way.

It's common for people to have an opinion because it makes them feel comfortable to think the way they do. Many philosophers dating back to Socrates have argued that, ultimately, all of our opinions are based on emotional factors.

Have any of your children ever tricked you into submitting to the infinite "why" trap? You tell your child that he should go to bed, and he asks, "why?" If you try to use it as a learning experience, you're trapped, because whatever explanation you use, will be followed by another "why," and that explanation with yet another. Ultimately, to escape the trap, you simply say, "because I told you to go to bed." But if you were completely honest, you'd have to admit that it's partly because it makes you feel good for him to go to bed, and that you'd feel bad for him to stay up.

Don't get me wrong. I believe in ultimate truth. and that logic and scientific evidence can help us understand it. But even scientists don't always agree on the interpretation of evidence, so truth ultimately becomes a very personal matter. And a person's emotional reaction to an opinion is always a very important factor.

I am a firm believer that two heads are better than one when it comes to discovering truth, particularly when one is a man and the other a woman. But in marriage, there is an ultimate advantage if a husband and wife respect each other's opinions. Both of them can learn from each other. They complement each other.

I'll give you an illustration of this point in the next section of this chapter. But for now, I simply want you to recognize that conflicting opinions in marriage are often due to conflicting emotional reactions. If emotional reactions are not respectfully addressed in marital negotiation, a resolution will be difficult, if not impossible, to find.

*Conflicting opinions in marriage are often due to conflicting emotional reactions. If emotional reactions are not respectfully addressed in marital negotiation, a resolution will be difficult, if not impossible, to find.*

In the first few weeks that I counseled Linda and Tom, she began to express her opinions more openly and spoke freely of her *feelings*. This was an eye-opener for Linda. Tom had been in the habit of justifying his decisions with his assumptions and logic. He would even support his assumptions with articles that he would try to force her to read. If she told him his decision did not "feel" right to her, he would attack her values and argue that values were more important than feelings, and that his conclusions logically followed from his assumptions which were supported by "fact." Previously she had bought into his arguments, and when his decisions made her unhappy, she had concluded that something was wrong with her.

But now Linda was coming to realize that Tom's assumptions were often nothing more than rationalizations of *his* feelings. She noticed that if his feelings about something changed, he could easily create a new set of assumptions and logic to accommodate them. Tom's feelings turned out to be more important than he had led her to believe.

So if you should not try to force your way of thinking on your spouse, should you try to change your spouse's mind at all?

Absolutely. In marriage, a husband and wife can learn quite a bit from each other, and changes in perspective are an important part of each spouse's personal growth. But if you wish to persuade your spouse to your way of thinking, you must first determine why your point of view would be an improvement for him or her. If your opinion would make life easier or more successful, then your appeal should be seriously considered. It would make your spouse feel good about the new opinion. But if it makes *your* life easier *at your spouse's expense* (which is often the case), your selfish motives will make your position very weak.

Persuasion begins with an understanding of the other person's needs, and an awareness of how a change in opinion can fulfill those needs. If it were demonstrated that a change in opinion would make the other person happier and more productive, it would be accepted with enthusiasm.

That sounds a little like the Policy of Joint Agreement, doesn't it? *Never do anything without an enthusiastic agreement between you and your spouse.* If you want to get something you haven't been getting from your spouse by changing your spouse's opinion on the issue, there must be something in it for him or her too.

If what you want is simply not in your spouse's best interest, just drop the subject and move on. But if you're certain that your opinion would be of value to your spouse, you need to introduce evidence to prove it. People are usually willing to try something for a while, and that may give you the chance to test the value of your opinion.

To explain this method, let me introduce the Three Steps to Respectful Persuasion.

### Three Steps to Respectful Persuasion

*Step 1: Clearly state your conflicting opinions to each other with an emphasis on emotional associations.*

To help Linda and Tom learn how to respectfully persuade each other, I asked them to think of an issue that they would like to tackle. They chose to discuss Tom's housework expectations and Linda's reluctance to meet them.

We could have chosen anything from a host of other examples of Tom's expectations that were not being fulfilled by Linda, because he felt she was shirking her duty as his wife in almost everything she did. But this was a good place to start because it would give both of them general guidelines in addressing the larger problem of Tom's disrespectful judgments.

When Tom began explaining his opinion, he talked about the responsibilities of a wife. But I wanted him to talk about it in emotional terms. So I encouraged him to try again, and this time to explain his emotional reactions rather than his rules for a wife.

That simple change helped both Tom and Linda gain a much greater insight into each other's opinions. Tom began to describe his feelings about homemaking rather than the rules that he applied to his wife. He described how he felt when the house was picked up, and how he felt when things were messy. Several other household issues were raised such as how the meals were prepared, the way the table was set, and how quickly the dishes were washed and put away.

Tom had an emotional need for domestic support (see chapter 16). He needed a home where everything would be in order when he came home from work: the house would be immaculate and dinner would be ready to serve. Whenever Linda would fulfill this need, which happened on rare occasion, he felt wonderful. And when it was unmet, he felt frustrated and unhappy.

Then it was Linda's turn. Her opinion began with a basic agreement with Tom's rules. She felt obligated to be the homemaker that he had wanted. But when I asked her to explain it in emotional terms, she described the guilt that she felt having failed to meet Tom's expectations. At first, she had wanted to be the perfect homemaker, but there was always something that he would find to be "out of place" or "wrong" about the way she did things. Then, Linda explained, since Tom was so critical of her housekeeping, she began to hate anything associated with it. She eventually developed an aversion to it. Now she hardly ever felt like cooking or cleaning.

The logical way to approach Tom's problem was to make the meeting of his need for domestic support enjoyable for Linda. But he had done the opposite: He had made it so unpleasant that now she hated meeting his need. Instead of appreciating her efforts, he was critical of them, telling her that they were not up to his standards.

### Step 2: Explain how your opinion is in your spouse's best interest.

I'm using the example of Tom and Linda's conflict over housekeeping to illustrate how often the needs of a husband or wife are translated into opinions when the needs are not met. Tom wanted Linda to meet his need for domestic support. When his demand that she meet his need didn't work, he added disrespectful judgments to his approach. He told her that she was not being a good wife because she was not following his rules. But his rules were nothing more than a misguided way of trying to motivate her to meet his need.

Tom had insisted on taking the position that Linda was responsibile to meet his emotional need for domestic support in the way he wanted it done. He tried to convince her that it was in her best interest to meet that need because she would be rewarded by God and that she would feel good knowing that he was happy.. But those arguments had not worked for her. All they did was make her feel guilty.

So Tom took my advice and focused his attention on how meeting his need would be in Linda's best interest from her perspective. He began by asking her how he could make the meeting of his need enjoyable for her.

If he had taken that approach early in their marriage, it would have been easier for her to answer. At that point, she wanted to meet whatever need he had, simply because she loved him. If he had been sensitive to her feelings, trying to be sure that her efforts were enjoyable for her and appreciated by him, she could have become everything he had ever hoped for in a homemaker. And she would have remained in love with him.

But now, with her aversion to doing housework, she couldn't think of anything that would make the experience enjoyable for her.

While an aversion may seem impossible to overcome at the time a person is experiencing it, reversing the associations that created it in the first place can do it. For Linda, housework had been associated with failure and criticism. If, instead, it was associated with achievement and admiration, the negative associations of the past would be replaced with positive associations. Over time, the aversion would disappear and she would feel good about doing housework.

If Tom had persisted in his original disrespectful approach to having Linda meet his need for domestic support, he would not have convinced her that it was in her best interest to do so. Instead, she would have been convinced that it was in her best interest to divorce him.

So to meet the conditions of the second step toward respectful persuasion, he had to find ways to reward her for her effort. *What could I do to make housekeeping enjoyable for Linda?* was the question that had to be answered.

### Step 3: Suggest a test of your opinion.

At this point in their discussion Tom had changed his opinion. Instead of feeling that Linda had an obligation to meet his housekeeping standards, whether she enjoyed it or not, he felt that she should meet his need only if she enjoyed doing it. And that she would enjoy it if she would give him a chance to prove it. Linda, on the other hand, had not changed her opinion. She still felt that she could never come up to his standards, that she could never enjoy housekeeping, and that she didn't want to try anymore.

People often make a big mistake in marital "discussions" when they try to force each other to make a commitment to a permanent change rather than to a temporary one. Linda was not convinced that she could ever enjoy housework. But Tom was not asking for a commitment to meet his need. He was only asking her to try a new approach to housework that she might enjoy. Her curiosity about the possibility that she might actually enjoy housework some day, and her respect for my advice, encouraged her to risk a test of Tom's new opinion. They would find some other way to have the housework done. So she expressed a willingness to try step 3: "Try it. You'll like it!"

Linda gave Tom a list of what she hated most about housekeeping and what she enjoyed most. On the top of her list of what she hated most was Tom's inspections, and his lectures. So he made a commitment to her that all of the disrespectful judgments he had made in the past would be completely eliminated by him in the future. He also asked her to complete a worksheet that I provided that gave her an opportunity to identify all instances of his disrespect. His goal was to see a blank sheet each week.

From Linda's original lists, they made up a new list of tasks that she enjoyed doing by herself, another list that she would enjoy if Tom were to do them with her, and a third list of unpleasant tasks that they set aside for a housekeeper to do.

Tom's willingness to do whatever it took to change Linda's opinion about housekeeping was the biggest part of the solution. But the end result also had to work well for Tom. In other words, both he and she had to be enthusiastic about the way it was working for them.

Some of the tasks that Linda wanted Tom to do with her were unpleasant for Tom. So they were either eliminated, or given to the housekeeper to do.

The first week turned out better than Linda had expected. But she was looking for any expressions of disappointment from Tom. When he would simply glance across the room when he first came home, she interpreted it as his judgment of her housekeeping. So he learned to look directly at her when he entered the front door, and give her a big hug and kiss. By the second week, she was more relaxed, and took his accolades at face value.

Overall, the plan worked very well, and what Linda had once seen as a hopeless task became an enjoyable way of life for her. Eventually, they had two children, and by applying what they had learned while respectfully persuading each other, Linda became a very satisfied homemaker, and Tom was happy with the way she managed the home for him.

## Some Unresolved Conflicts of Opinion Are Inevitable

At this point in our discussion, you may be wondering what to do if your test doesn't work. What if Linda had not changed her opinion about being unable to meet Tom's expectations after the test? What if Tom continued to feel disappointed in the way she was completing her household tasks?

Their options at that point would be to try another test, or to drop the subject. What was learned with the first test? Can modifications be made to make a second test more likely to succeed? If you are both willing to try again, the outcome may be different.

But I want you to be aware of a very important fact—you do not have to change each other's minds about something in order to create behavior that makes each other happy. Remember, it's what you do *for* each other that will make you happy, or what you do *to* each other that will make you unhappy. So in your efforts to create a more passionate marriage, one where you'll find each other absolutely irresistible, your attention should be focused more on each other's habits than on each other's beliefs, opinions, and attitudes.

In the case of Linda and Tom, meeting his need for domestic support was not absolutely essential for them to have a very happy marriage. If he would simply stop making disrespectful judgments about her housekeeping, and about everything else she did, her ability to meet his other emotional needs could have blossomed. His criticism of her caused her to erect a defensive wall around herself, preventing her from meeting any of his intimate emotional needs, such as sexual fulfillment and affection. When that wall came down, she would not necessarily have been the best housekeeper, but she could have been the best romantic partner for him.

> *You do not have to change each other's minds about something in order to create behavior that makes each other happy.*

## Are You a Disrespectful Judge or a Respectful Persuader?

In the last chapter, I encouraged you to answer the questions on the disrespectful judgments page of the Love Busters Questionnaire (page 213). The answers to those questions will help you identify disrespectful judgments that may have invaded your marriage.

But there is another way to know if you're a perpetrator of disrespectful judgments. Ask your spouse to answer the following questions with a number rating from 1 to 10. A 1 means "never" while a 10 means "always." The numbers in between reflect various levels of disrespect.

1. Does your spouse ever try to straighten you out?
2. Does your spouse ever lecture you instead of respectfully discussing issues?
3. Does your spouse seem to feel that his or her opinion is superior to yours?
4. When you and your spouse discuss an issue, does he or she interrupt you or talk so much it prevents you from having a chance to explain your position?
5. Does your spouse ever ridicule your opinions or behavior?

The scoring of this questionnaire is simple. Unless all your spouse's answers are 1, you're probably engaging in at least some disrespectful judgments. Almost all of us are guilty of this from time to time, so don't be alarmed if you get some 2s or 3s. But if your spouse gave you any 4s, 5s, 6s, or 7s, you're probably at risk of losing some of the romantic love in your marriage.

If your spouse identifies you as one who makes disrespectful judgments, you'll probably be tempted to make yet another disrespectful judgment and claim that he or she is wrong! Trust me, in this situation your spouse is the best judge of this common problem in marriage.

An important part of romantic relationships is the support and encouragement lovers show each other. Disrespectful judgments do the opposite. If they have crept into your marriage, make an effort today to eliminate their destructive influence.

Imposing your point of view is bad enough. But when your point of view criticizes your spouse's character or value, you're making the biggest disrespectful judgment of all. If you ever hope to be in a romantic relationship with your spouse again, you must avoid critical generalizations at all costs.

## Measure Your Progress

Whatever your goal is in life, it makes sense to measure your progress toward it. Are you making progress? How will you know when you've been successful?

I recommend using two worksheets to hold each other accountable and to measure your progress. Title one "Disrespectful Judgments Worksheet," and the other, "Respectful Persuasion Worksheet."

The Disrespectful Judgments Worksheet should list each disrespectful judgment by the day, date, and time that it was made, with a brief description of what was said and the circumstances surrounding it. The Respectful Persuasion Worksheet should record the same information when an effort toward respectful persuasion is made.

The spouse who is the recipient of disrespectful judgments is to complete both worksheets, and is the final judge as to what is and what isn't a disrespectful judgment and respectful persuasion.

Your goal is to completely eliminate any instance of a disrespectful judgment, and to fill the Respectful Persuasion Worksheet each week. When you and your spouse are both satisfied that the habit of making disrespectful judgments has been replaced with the habit of making respectful persuasion, you will no longer need to use these worksheets. But because habits are hard to break, plan on keeping these records for at least three months.

## Key Principles

Opinions should be expressed in both propositional and emotional terms. In other words, explain how your opinion makes you feel.

**The Three Steps to Respectful Persuasion are:**

Step 1  Clearly state your conflicting opinions to each other with an emphasis on emotional associations.

Step 2  Explain how your opinion is in your spouse's best interest.

Step 3  Suggest a test of your opinion.

Hold yourself accountable with the Disrespectful Judgments Worksheet and the Respectful Persuasion Worksheet.

# *Consider This . . .* _____

1. Are you both willing to completely eliminate disrespectful judgments? If you are in the habit of being disrespectful, it will take practice to avoid it. I recommend completing the Disrespectful Judgments Worksheet and the Respectful Persuasion Worksheet each week. When your spouse completes the Disrespectful Judgments Worksheet, remember, the one who feels you have been disrespectful has an important point to make and you should try to understand it. It's up to you to change your approach so that it is interpreted by your spouse as being respectful.

2. How skilled are you in trying to persuade each other? When spouses are in the habit of being disrespectful, they are often reluctant to try to change each other's minds as often as they should. They tend to use disrespect as a last resort to getting what they think they deserve, and forget about trying to persuade each other to get what they need. Follow the Three Steps to Respectful Persuasion to gain insight into each other's opinions and to influence those opinions. By learning how to respectfully persuade, you will probably challenge each other's opinions and behavior more often, and receive more wisdom from each other than you did when you were being disrespectful.

# 8

## Angry Outbursts: *Part 1*

### Who Wants to Live with a Time Bomb?

Jill's father was kind and generous 99 percent of the time. But during that other 1 percent, he terrorized the entire household with his anger. So even though Jill's boyfriend, Sam, lost his temper once in a while, she considered him well-mannered compared to her father's outrageous behavior. Sam didn't hit anyone, he didn't break furniture, and he was never arrested for disorderly conduct—he was a real gentleman!

Before they married, Sam directed his anger away from Jill. He'd curse other drivers on the road, he'd fume over his boss's foolish decisions, and he'd become irate when salespeople failed to wait on him quickly. Jill did many of the same things, so she just chalked this up to human nature.

One morning soon after they were married, both Sam and Jill over-slept and were running late. As they scurried about, getting dressed, Sam suddenly had a problem.

"Jill, I'm out of clean shirts," he shouted.

She didn't quite know how to respond. Since they both worked, Jill and Sam usually "shared" the washing and ironing of clothes, but they had come to no formal understanding about who did what.

Like most people with anger problems, Sam was a very generous person. He would go out of his way to help others, especially Jill. So most of the time, "sharing" meant that he would do all of the washing and ironing. He wasn't happy about it, but didn't say anything until that fateful morning.

Jill tried to lighten up the situation. "I don't think any of mine will fit you," she joked.

"Was that supposed to be funny?" Sam shot back.

"Wear the one you wore yesterday," Jill suggested, trying to be helpful.

But Sam had already decided that she was at fault. "You had to notice that I was out of shirts last night," he bellowed.

"Me, notice your shirts? Please, get serious." With that she turned to finish getting ready herself.

"I'm not done talking to you. You knew I was out of shirts, didn't you?"

"No," she said, "I didn't know you were out of shirts. But even if I did, it's your problem, not mine."

With that, Sam flew into a rage, complete with recriminations, condemnations, and obscenities.

Jill started to cry. This was the first time Sam had directed his anger toward her. Although he was not being physically violent, it hurt her deeply. Sam left the room, and nothing more was said about the incident.

This angry outburst was the first of many Jill would endure during the first year of their marriage. The pattern would always be the same: Sam would have a problem, assume that Jill should have done something to solve it, and when she did not, he would lose his temper. Then she would cry, and he would back off. As time passed, however, the frequency and intensity of these outbursts increased.

They were planning to have children, but Jill wisely chose to see a marriage counselor first. She was afraid Sam's anger would eventually turn into the mayhem she had witnessed as a child.

Jill was wise to see a marriage counselor for another reason. Sam's angry outbursts had punched a hole in her Love Bank—it had sprung a leak. After one year of marriage, she was losing her feeling of love for Sam.

Every time Sam lost his temper, he was punishing Jill. This was doubly painful for Jill—she not only suffered from his punishing anger but also from the shocking realization that he was *trying* to hurt her. The man who had committed himself to her protection had become her greatest threat.

Why do couples destroy the love they have for each other with angry outbursts? In most cases, the problem begins with the false assumption that their spouse should do this or that for them. And when they don't face up to their responsibilities, they should be forced to do the right thing.

Control is ultimately behind every angry outburst. And when a spouse does not do what is expected (selfish demands), recriminations usually follow. Sam accused Jill of being an uncaring person because she didn't wash and iron his shirts. That's a disrespectful judgment. Then, when she didn't respond properly to his accusations, his angry outburst was justified as punishment for her attitude.

An angry outburst is usually an effort to teach a lesson—the one partner feels hurt and angrily tries to show the other how that feels. But in most cases, the angry spouse does not expect this punishment to ruin their love—after all, they promised to love each other forever.

They may have made the promise, but it was one they couldn't keep. People's feelings for each other are determined not by promises but by the Love Bank. When couples deliberately try to hurt each other, they deplete their Love Bank accounts. Romantic love becomes the victim of their anger.

### Escalating Control and Abuse

So far in this book I've introduced you to two types of Love Busters, selfish demands and disrespectful judgments. I've discussed them in this sequence because they represent an escalation of control and abuse in marriage. Remember, control is forcing your spouse to do what you want, and abuse is hurting your spouse intentionally. Neither of these should be tolerated in marriage.

Control and abuse usually begin with selfish demands, because they are attempts to force your spouse to do something for you that he or she is reluctant to do. In other words, you're trying to gain at your spouse's expense. You're willing to let your spouse suffer to get what you want.

The next level of control and abuse in most marriages is disrespectful judgments. In fact, they usually come on the heels of a failed selfish demand. If you can't force your spouse to do what you want with a demand, then you escalate the control and abuse with disrespectful judgments.

If you stop to analyze the fights between you and your spouse, I think you'll see what I mean. You'll find that they often begin with demands, and from there disrespectful judgments quickly follow. And if you don't have the sense to stop arguing, the Love Buster I'll introduce to you in this chapter, angry outbursts, is sure to rear its ugly head. It's usually the final stage in the escalation of control and abuse, where a spouse deliberately does all he or she can to hurt the other in a fit of rage.

## Anger: A Threat to Your Spouse's Safety

I've listened to husbands swear never to hit their wives again, but by the next time I see them, they've inflicted even more bruises. One man I counseled, who claimed to be "cured" of his violent tendencies in a religious service, tried to kill his wife a short time later. Another man attempted to kill his wife three times before she finally divorced him upon my recommendation. After each attempt on his wife's life, including the last, it was determined by counselors that it was safe for his wife to return to him.

I have witnessed many cases of murdered and permanently injured men and women who gave their spouse one chance too many. That's why my approach to domestic violence is extremely cautious, and often requires separation while an angry spouse is learning to control his or her temper. Even then I remain cautious, usually recommending continued separation until selfish demands and disrespectful judgments have also been eliminated, as well as angry outbursts. I want proof that all vestiges of control and abuse have been eliminated before I consider the marriage to be safe.

Your anger is the greatest threat to your spouse's safety. Even if you've never been physically violent, and have limited your angry outbursts to verbal tirades, emotional abuse can be extremely damaging. And there's no assurance that you will not resort to physical violence for the first time during one of your fights. But you risk more than physical or emotional harm during an angry outburst: You risk losing your spouse's love for you. Without a doubt it's a Love Buster.

When you're angry, hurting others seems reasonable. They have caused you to be unhappy, and they'll keep upsetting you until they're punished. They can't be reasoned with; the only thing they understand is pain and personal loss. Once you inflict that punishment, they'll think twice about making you unhappy again!

> *Your anger is the greatest threat to your spouse's safety.*

Anger's solution to a problem is to punish the troublemaker. This emotion overrides intelligence, which knows that punishment usually doesn't solve problems (at least for adults); it only makes the people you punish angry, which causes them to inflict punishment on you.

Most of the people that I've counseled who are perpetrators of angry outbursts don't see their anger as a serious problem in their marriage. As far as they're concerned, the real problem is their spouse's behavior that they think triggers their angry outbursts. "If she'd just stop being so annoying, I wouldn't get angry." "If he'd be a little more thoughtful and considerate I wouldn't lose my temper." In other words, most of the people who have angry outbursts feel that the other person made them do it.

## Generosity Can Lead to Angry Outbursts

Angry spouses tend to feel that the other spouse just isn't treating them fairly. Some of their feeling of injustice comes from the fact that they don't believe that they should have to negotiate to get what they need. They feel that whatever is needed by either spouse should be freely given by each other, sacrificially if necessary. Why negotiate when you should simply do whatever is necessary to please each other? But when the other spouse doesn't do whatever they wish, they feel cheated and unloved.

As I already mentioned, Sam was a generous man. But his generosity helped cause his resentment. When Jill needed something, he would give it to her, and he expected her to give him whatever he needed. He expected her to notice that his shirt inventory was down, drop whatever she was doing, and get right to work washing and ironing shirts. Sam felt that he would do the same for Jill if the roles were reversed—because he cared about her.

Don't get me wrong. I care enough about my wife, Joyce, to sacrifice my life for her. And she feels the same about me. But we care enough about each other to refuse that offer. We don't want the other person to lose for our personal benefit. When we need something from each other we try to get it in a way that benefits both of us through negotiation.

It's the difference between individual care and mutual care. I can willingly sacrifice individually for anyone that doesn't care about me. But in a relationship of mutual care, the other person should not let me do it. Instead, we should work together to find ways to care for each other in mutually beneficial ways.

Sacrifice or capitulation on the part of either spouse for the sake of the other means that someone is being uncaring. Why would a caring spouse want the other to lose for his or her benefit? The one accepting the other spouse's loss would have to be uncaring at that moment. That's why a couple who cares about each other should meet each other's needs in ways that do not require loss.

*If spouses give unconditionally without negotiating, they create incompatibility and resentment.*

When sacrifices in marriage are not reciprocated, it usually makes people, like Sam, feel very resentful. They think they have a right to feel angry, because an obligation was not fulfilled. But the very nature of generosity doesn't create an obligation at all—it does not require reciprocity. In fact, when we do something for our spouse out of generosity, it should be assumed that he or she doesn't have to do anything in return for our sacrifice.

There are many who encourage spouses to give unconditionally to each other. But that advice fails to take the value of marital negotiation into account. Through negotiation, spouses can find conditions that lead to win-win solutions to their problems. That helps them grow in compatibility and love for each other. But if they give unconditionally without negotiating, they create incompatibility and resentment.

I think you can see the problem that Sam and Jill faced. Unspoken expectations and a failure to negotiate mutually enthusiastic agreements led to Sam's resentment and that, in turn, convinced him that his angry outburst was justified. There's a sense in which Sam's generosity ultimately created the seeds for the destruction of their relationship. By being generous, he failed to understand the importance of negotiation, and that failure could have ended their marriage.

## The Right to Control Can Lead to Angry Outbursts

Many, like Sam, are angry because they feel that they're being treated unfairly. But there are others who feel that they have the right to control the other, and are angry when the other does not submit. A husband may believe that his wife should obey his commands, and if he does not discipline her when she refuses, she will not be the wife that she should be. A wife may feel that her husband lacks good judgment, and unless she takes things into her own hands and forces the issue, the family will ultimately suffer.

Many of those I've counseled don't see that they're doing anything wrong when they try to force their spouse to do what they want. They feel they have that right, and with it, they have the right to have an angry outburst.

These are people who are particularly difficult to convince that their angry outbursts are destroying the love that their spouse has for them. And even if they know that they risk losing that love, they feel that control is more important than romantic love in marriage. Besides, they reason, their spouse promised to be in love with them as part of their wedding vow. It's their spouse's responsibility to love them.

This line of reasoning, of course, is not supported by fact. Romantic love is a reaction to the way we are treated. We can't decide with whom we will be in love.

## An Angry Outburst Is Temporary Insanity

An angry outburst has all of the characteristics of an emotional break-down. Paranoid thinking with delusional beliefs, an emotionally charged state of mind with excessive but poorly focused energy, and a profound inability to accurately remember what really takes place. As a couple tries to explain to me what happened during their last fight, it seems as if they did not experience the same event. They accuse each other of lying, when they actually can't remember. Their brains try to fill in the blanks in absence of accurate memory.

Angry outbursts are so common that people tend to consider them a part of normal living. But just because they exist for so many people doesn't make them safe or rational. The momentary insanity of an angry outburst is just as dangerous as some of the most well-recognized psychotic disorders. But because they don't last very long, they are not usually taken as seriously as they should be.

I have asked some of the couples I counsel to bring me sound or video recordings of their fights. They listen and watch them with me, and are horrified by what they hear and see themselves doing. What their memory didn't record is seen for the first time. It doesn't take much convincing on my part to prove to them that they were insane during the fight.

## Angry Outbursts Should Never Be Tolerated

There are reasons for angry outbursts, but there are no excuses. Whatever causes one spouse to feel justified in blasting away at the other, its outcome is always the same: it causes pain and suffering to the person that you promised to love and cherish. Instead of evening the score, or solving the problem, it withdraws love units. Your angry outburst causes your spouse to love you less. And anger is so unpredictable and so dangerous that you shouldn't even live with your spouse until you can guarantee his or her emotional and physical protection.

I've recommended separation for many of the spouses that I've counseled for angry outbursts when they cannot control their temper. As I mentioned, when you're angry, you are not simply upset—you're insane. You are not reasoning correctly. You think the way paranoid people think—that your spouse is your enemy and is deliberately trying to hurt you. Any effort that your spouse makes to reason with you is rebuffed. You are dangerous.

Even therapy that is ultimately successful does not suddenly end abusive acts. It usually brings about only a gradual decrease in angry outbursts. This can sometimes be tolerated if we were dealing with, say, name-calling. An occasional slipup like that during the therapeutic process will not usually threaten the safety of a spouse. But it's quite another matter when the occasional failure takes the form of a violent act, even if it's not physical.

I offer a plan to overcome angry outbursts in the next chapter. And in some cases, the plan can be followed without the need for separation. But if the arsenal of weapons you use during an angry outburst puts your spouse in physical or emotional danger, I strongly suggest immediate separation, and to follow the plan while separated. You will most certainly have failures from time to time as you overcome this abusive habit, and if you live together, that failure can cost your spouse permanent injury or even death. Only when your spouse's physical and emotional safety can be guaranteed should you live with each other again. You should adopt a zero-tolerance policy toward angry outbursts.

I hope you agree with me that an angry outburst in any form makes you temporarily insane and leaves your spouse unprotected. No one should have to put up with your angry outbursts, especially your spouse. So if you've decided to end your verbal or physical attacks on your spouse once and for all, you're a good candidate for my plan to completely eliminate angry outbursts.

## Key Principles

An **angry outburst** is a deliberate attempt to hurt your spouse because of anger, usually in the form of verbal or physical attacks.

When selfish demands and disrespectful judgments fail to get you what you need from your spouse, you'll be tempted to use angry outbursts as your next approach to solving the problem. It is the third and final escalation of abuse and control as a strategy for getting your way.

Angry spouses are often generous spouses. But when their sacrifice for their spouse is not reciprocated, they feel that their spouse should be punished.

Angry spouses often feel that they have the right to be controlling and abusive. They don't feel that they are doing anything wrong when they lose their temper in an attempt to gain control.

An angry outburst is temporary insanity, and the direction it takes is unpredictable. Permanent physical damage and even murder can occur during an angry outburst where the risk had not been apparent prior to the episode. This is an important reason why couples should have no tolerance for angry outbursts.

## Consider This . . .

1. Are angry outbursts a problem in your marriage? To answer that question, complete the angry outbursts page (page 214) of the Love Busters Questionnaire in Appendix B. Make two enlarged copies, one for each of you, so that you will have enough space to write your answers.

2. When one of you has an angry outburst, does the other spouse bring it to his or her attention? What have the consequences of such feedback been? Do you tend to punish each other for complaining about angry outbursts, or do you appreciate the feedback?

3. Describe your arsenal of weapons. What do you tend to do when you have an angry outburst? Which weapons are the most offensive to your spouse?

4. Do you take full responsibility for your angry outbursts, or do you blame them on your spouse? Remember, you will not be able to overcome your angry outbursts until you realize that you, and only you, can control them.

# 9

## Angry Outbursts: *Part 2*

### How to Overcome Angry Outbursts

Sam was not so sure he had a problem with angry outbursts. That's a common perspective of those who can't seem to control their temper.

Anger is deceitful: it lets you forget what really happened and offers you a distortion of the truth. When Jill described one of Sam's angry outbursts to me, he shook his head in disbelief. "It just didn't happen that way," he said in all sincerity. "I don't understand why you would tell Dr. Harley such a thing."

Of course, I wasn't at the scene, but experience has taught me to give the benefit of the doubt to the victim. As I mentioned earlier, I view an angry outburst as a form of temporary insanity. What is said and done is often about as irrational as a psychotic episode, and when it is recorded, the one having the angry outburst usually agrees with my assessment once he or she hears and sees themselves in action.

The fact that the details of the angry outburst are often forgotten or remembered falsely is also typical of a psychotic episode. Insane behavior usually takes a detour around our intelligence and causes us to behave in primitive and irrational ways. Then it either fails to give us any memory of what we did or gives us an inaccurate memory that makes the outburst seem more rational than it was.

Anger is deceitful and cunning: it tries to convince you that an angry outburst is caused by someone else's behavior. Sam felt that Jill "made him" angry. If she had been more considerate, he would not have lost his temper. So it was her fault.

Many of my violent clients, both men and women, have told me that they had no choice but to lose their temper. Besides, their spouses had it coming to them. They deserved the angry reaction.

How do you go about stripping anger's deceit and cunning from outbursts so that anger can be seen for what it is? It's an ugly monster. How do you remove the screen that it hides behind?

## Six Steps to Overcoming Angry Outbursts

### Step 1: Acknowledge the fact that you, and you only, determine if you will have an angry outburst. No one "makes" you angry.

What a place to begin. Sam was thoroughly convinced that Jill made him angry, and that there was little he could do to avoid his angry outbursts. *If Jill would be more thoughtful*, he reasoned, *I would be less angry*. How could I convince Sam that he could completely overcome angry outbursts without Jill making any change in her behavior? And to go one step further, how could I convince him that unless he took full responsibility for his angry outbursts, he could not learn to control them?

I think that I'm a good counselor for those with anger problems, because I have had a history of angry outbursts myself. When I was growing up, I lived with parents who had serious anger issues, and I suffered many beatings, especially at the hands of my mother. I expressed my own frustration with anger, and was in many physical fights with my peers.

But, like Sam, I never lost my temper with Joyce while I was dating her. I knew I was on thin ice, and she would certainly not put up with anger. So I was able to keep it under control—when I was with her.

One day I had an epiphany. I was replacing a transmission in my car, and it slipped out of my grasp and fell on top of me. I promptly lost my temper, and tried to destroy just about everything in sight, including the transmission. I was actually thinking that the transmission had fallen on me just to upset me. And everything else was somehow also involved. By the time I had a chance to calm down, I had put quite a few dents in the car, but the transmission itself was as good as new. It's hard to wreck a transmission with your bare hands.

As I looked at what I had done, and the reason that I did it, I realized that I had become temporarily insane. The transmission couldn't possibly have decided to drop on me. I let it slip. It was my fault. And yet, I blamed the transmission.

It was at that moment that I came to realize that I was insane whenever I lost my temper. And when I became angry with a person, I was dangerous. The transmission had nothing to fear, but I could hurt another person. And if that person were Joyce, I would be making the mistake of a lifetime.

So I made a decision that very day that I would not lose my temper again. At first, it took quite a bit of effort to avoid being angry. But eventually, I didn't even have to think about it. When I found myself in a frustrating situation, I rarely felt angry, and I never lost my temper. And that's the way I feel today.

How did I do it? The first step was realizing that only I was responsible for my angry outbursts, and that I could avoid them if I chose.

Over my lifetime, I've counseled scores of men with very serious problems with angry outbursts. Many of these men spent time in prison due to violent acts committed while they were angry. And I always begin their plan of recovery with their acknowledgment that no one "makes" them angry—that they are completely responsible for their angry outbursts.

On a related subject, some anger management therapists today agree that we are all responsible for our anger. But many feel that our anger is caused by our poor self-esteem. If we were to feel better about ourselves, we would not feel as angry. I want to warn you in the strongest terms to reject that reasoning for two reasons.

First, the angriest people I've ever counseled have high self-esteem, not low self-esteem. They feel entitled to whatever they want, and get angry with those who don't give it to them. There is considerable research on this subject that points to improved self-esteem as *increasing* angry outbursts, not decreasing them.

> *As soon as you give yourself any excuses for your angry outbursts— other people, the way you were raised, or even your poor self-esteem— you will not overcome your angry outbursts.*

Second, as soon as you give yourself any excuses for your angry outbursts—other people, the way you were raised, or even your poor self-esteem—you will not overcome your angry outbursts. That's because any excuse will sidetrack you from the best way to learn to control your temper, and that begins with accepting full responsibility for your actions. The remaining steps I recommend will help you completely eliminate this Love Buster regardless of who you're with, how you were raised, or any problems you may have with self-esteem.

### Step 2: Identify instances of your angry outbursts and their effects.

After I was able to convince Sam that he, and only he, could control his temper, we had another question to face: Did he have a problem with anger or didn't he? That may seem like a strange second step in my plan for recovery, but I know firsthand how deceitful anger can be. For the one losing his temper, it can seem like a simple expression of frustration. For the one on the receiving end, however, it can be a frightening display of insanity.

So I had to help Sam see his anger for what it really was—a monster. And the person in the best position to describe the effect of his anger was his wife, Jill.

I asked Jill to answer the following questions:

1. Using a scale of 0 to 6, with 0 indicating no unhappiness and 6 indicating extreme unhappiness, what number most accurately reflects how much unhappiness you tend to experience when your spouse attacks you with an angry outburst?
2. How often does your spouse tend to attack you with an angry outburst?

3. When your spouse attacks you with an angry outburst, what does he or she typically do? List the ways you are attacked.
4. Which of the ways you are attacked cause you the greatest unhappiness?
5. When did your spouse first attack you with an angry outburst?
6. Have your spouse's angry outbursts increased or decreased in intensity and/or frequency since they first began? How do recent angry outbursts compare with those of the past?

These are the same questions that you were to have answered on the angry outbursts page in Appendix B (page 214). If you answer these questions, you will know whether or not angry outbursts have invaded your marriage.

I've counseled many who, after reading their spouse's answers to these questions, simply laugh. They are amazed that their spouse would write down what they believe are lies about their behavior. The deceit and cunning of their anger blind them to the truth. In some cases, they even lose their tempers as they are reading the answers.

If your spouse answers these questions and you are tempted to view them as sheer fantasy, remember what I said about anger's deceit and cunning. Your spouse is in a much better position to record what you do when you are angry, so accept his or her word for it at this stage of the program. You must see anger for what it is: a threat to the safety and security of your spouse—and your marriage.

Jill's answers to these questions defined the problem and made it clear that Sam was making her unhappy with his angry outbursts. That was reason enough to do something about it. As Sam and I looked over Jill's answers, tears came to his eyes.

Sam saw that Jill had rated her unhappiness a 6, "extremely unhappy." He didn't want her to be unhappy and certainly didn't want to be the cause of her unhappiness.

What he had seen as an honest expression of his frustration she interpreted as an ambush, a painful attack. His method of communicating his feelings had turned him into her worst enemy.

Sam's vicious attacks on Jill's character and perspective (disrespectful judgments) were weaved into his angry outbursts. He would tell her how selfish she was, how he was doing everything for her and she was doing nothing for him. He also would berate her abilities, charging that her only value was in her figure, not in her head.

She felt his rantings simply weren't true. From her perspective, she did many things to prove her care for him and she was a highly skilled legal secretary, in great demand because of her knowledge and clerical ability. Sam's angry outbursts were filled with irrational statements made to hurt her, not to solve his problem.

Jill described the shirt incident as the first time she felt attacked by his angry outbursts. She had been a witness to his anger prior to that incident but until then it had not been directed toward her. She went on to describe his recent attacks and how they had become more frequent and more abusive since the shirt episode. Jill also said that she was unwilling to raise children in an environment overshadowed by the threat of violence.

After Sam finished reading Jill's answers to the questions, he agreed that he had an anger problem that should be overcome. He made no excuses and, for once, agreed with her interpretation of the problem. We were ready to go to the next step.

### Step 3: Understand why your angry outbursts take place.

Now it was Sam's turn to answer a few questions. Why did he lose his temper? I gave him the following questions to answer before our next appointment.

1. What are the most important reasons that you use angry outbursts to punish your spouse?
2. When you use angry outbursts to punish your spouse, what do you typically do?
3. When you use angry outbursts to punish your spouse, what hurts your spouse the most?

4. After you use angry outbursts to punish your spouse, do you usually feel better about the situation than before you used them? Why or why not?

5. Do you feel that punishment evens the score, and that without it your spouse wins and you lose? Explain.

6. Do you ever try to control or avoid using angry outbursts to punish your spouse? If so, why do you do it? How do you do it?

7. If you were to decide never to use angry outbursts to punish your spouse again, would you be able to stop? Why or why not?

8. Are you willing to stop using angry outbursts to punish your spouse? Why or why not?

There is something about all of these questions that should jump out at you. Do you see it? Each question assumes that angry outbursts are *intended* to be a punishment. As it turns out, one of the ways people deceive themselves about anger is to interpret it as something other than punishment. One of my clients called it an expression of his creativity; another viewed anger as a cry for help. I probably haven't heard them all but I've heard hundreds of ways that perpetrators of violence have downplayed what anger really is. It's punishment, pure and simple.

The purpose of angry outbursts is to inflict pain and suffering on the target. Any other interpretation is part of anger's deception. When the deception is removed and you see it for what it is—punishment—it's much easier to ask the question *why?*

Sam understood that he was punishing Jill whenever she was the target of his anger. As he answered the questions in the privacy of his home, he began to uncover the reasons. After they were married, he had a growing feeling that she was more important to him than he was to her. He was very generous with her, but he did not see the same generosity returned by her. He made sacrifices for her regularly, but she did not make the same sacrifices for him.

And her career seemed to be the most important thing in her life. His feelings were hurt whenever she made her work a higher priority than his interests. So whenever he lost his temper, he usually attacked her career, which he felt was coming between them. But he also attacked Jill.

As we went through his answers, he realized that he was using anger to even the score, to make her feel some of the pain he felt. He admitted that after an outburst he felt a little better. At least he had expressed his frustration instead of keeping it bottled inside of him.

After Sam made the commitment to control his temper, he didn't think it would be difficult to achieve. He would just have to make the decision to stop and that would be that. Most people with angry outbursts feel that way. Some are right, but time would tell if Sam was being realistic.

He had seen the error of his ways and he had decided to change. But was that enough?

### Step 4: Try to avoid the conditions that make angry outbursts difficult to control.

Before Sam left my office, I gave him a few more questions to answer for our next session. They concerned the angry outbursts we had been discussing in the assignment he had just completed:

1. In the instances of angry outbursts that you identified earlier, describe the conditions that seem to make angry outbursts difficult to control. Include your physical condition (amount of sleep, physical health, etc.), setting, people present and behavior of those people, your mental state, and any other relevant information.
2. What changes in any of those conditions or efforts to avoid those conditions might help you avoid angry outbursts in the future?
3. What changes identified in question 2 can be made with your spouse's enthusiastic agreement?
4. Describe your plan, which can be made with your spouse's enthusiastic agreement, to change or avoid the conditions. Include a deadline that also meets with his or her enthusiastic agreement.

Almost all of the conditions that tend to make angry outbursts more difficult to control usually begin with two very serious mistakes. The first mistake is to assume that caring people make sacrifices for each other. Remember the Policy of Joint Agreement? *Don't do anything without an enthusiastic agreement between you and your spouse.* That means if you're doing something for your spouse that you regard as a sacrifice, you're not following the Policy. Caring couples consider how they both feel simultaneously, and neither spouse expects or wants the other to suffer for them. It's only when we are uncaring that we expect our spouse to make sacrifices on our behalf.

But the problem goes beyond making sacrifices. It's also a misunderstanding regarding agreements. The person prone to angry outbursts often feels that there's an unspoken understanding—if I do this for you, you'll do this for me. But when that agreement isn't made clear and isn't understood by the other spouse, disappointment is sure to follow. So one of the lessons Sam learned was that he should not only avoid making sacrifices for Jill, but he should also be sure that agreements were clearly understood by both of them.

> *Caring couples consider how they both feel simultaneously, and neither spouse expects or wants the other to suffer for them.*

Another lesson Sam learned was that his angry outburst often came at the end of an argument that should never have taken place. The argument would begin with a demand—telling Jill what to do. When she was unwilling to comply with the demand, he would say something disrespectful, and if that didn't work, out came his arsenal of weapons.

He also learned that he could lose his temper if Jill demanded something of him, followed by disparaging remarks if he didn't comply. It can seem reasonable to respond with an angry outburst when your spouse threatens you for failing to deliver on his or her demand.

So an angry outburst can be a tempting reaction to your spouse's demand of you. By eliminating demands altogether in your marriage, you'll be getting rid of a very important condition that makes angry outbursts more difficult to control.

The same thing can be said for disrespectful judgments. If your spouse says something disrespectful about you, you may feel tempted to respond with an angry outburst. By overcoming disrespectful judgments in your marriage, again, you eliminate one of the important conditions that make it more difficult to control an angry outburst.

Another condition that may challenge your ability to control your temper is your physical state of mind. You may find, for example, that when you wake up in the morning you tend to become frustrated with very little provocation. Low blood sugar can be the culprit, and breakfast may be all it takes for you to pull yourself together and gain control of yourself. If that's the case, your first item of business every morning should be to have breakfast.

Physical surroundings may also affect your temptation to lose your temper. For example, battling traffic on your way home from work may put you in such a foul mood that nobody would want to have dinner with you, especially your spouse. So either changing your work schedule or changing the route you take to get home might make a world of difference in the attitude that you have most evenings.

You'll find that if you create a lifestyle around the Policy of Joint Agreement, where the events of your day are compatible with both your sensitivities and the sensitivities of your spouse, you'll greatly reduce the conditions that tend to frustrate you.

When a husband and wife come to an agreement, I want it to be an *enthusiastic* one. Halfhearted, self-sacrificing arrangements generally fall apart the first time they're tested. So any changes that would help Sam control his temper had to be agreed to enthusiastically by Jill.

Sam felt that mornings were worst for him and that he tended to wake up irritable. Little things that Jill would do or say bothered him terribly at that time of the day. Later in the day, he seemed to have a completely different outlook on life and he could handle irritations much better.

Jill's job was Sam's greatest source of frustration. Whenever she talked about it, particularly when she talked about her boss, it drove him nuts. He saw her job in general and her boss in particular as great threats to their future. Sam was fearful that Jill would eventually have an affair with her boss.

It is quite common for jealous husbands or wives to be angry with their spouse. The threat of something or someone coming between them makes them furious. Their anger, of course, doesn't begin to solve the problem. In fact it tends to drive their spouse into the arms of anyone who will save him or her from their terror experienced in marriage. Whether or not Sam had anything to fear from Jill's boss, his anger greatly increased the risk of an affair.

Angry outbursts make the solution to marital problems much more difficult to find. The conflict that Sam had with Jill over her work and her relationship with her boss could have been resolved through thoughtful negotiation. But Sam's angry outbursts ruined that possibility.

So I encouraged Sam to resolve his conflict with Jill *after* he had learned to control his temper, rather than making it a *condition* to control his temper. It's like negotiating with terrorists. Whatever they demand, you cannot let them have it. They must remove the threat to innocent citizens before you discuss a resolution. Otherwise they will use that threat every time they want something.

Sam's early-morning irritability was another matter entirely. Jill was perfectly willing to avoid discussing conflicts with him in the morning, and Sam also agreed. So they decided that their morning conversation would be limited to "please pass the orange juice," avoiding any unpleasant topics. And he followed my advice to have breakfast as soon as possible in the morning.

### Step 5: Train yourself to control your temper when you cannot avoid frustrating situations.

It may seem to you that in Step 4 I'm backtracking on what I said in Step 1. In other words, it may seem that I don't really think that angry outbursts are completely within our control, because I focus on outside conditions in Step 4. But Step 5 should straighten out that misconception. While the first line of defense against angry outbursts should be to try to avoid conditions that are frustrating, I am a witness to the fact that even when these conditions cannot be avoided, you should know how to control your temper. If your spouse seems uncooperative, or if he or she refuses to stop making demands, being disrespectful, or having angry outbursts, or if he or she continues to do the things that irritate you most, you can control your temper even under those conditions. I've found that when a person simply can't avoid frustrating situations, the best way to keep their cabinet of weapons locked up is to physically relax.

For someone with a history of angry outbursts, that solution may sound really stupid at first. How can you relax when you are faced with a spouse who keeps badgering you, ridiculing you, and has their own problems with anger? I've had many spouses tell me that they try to avoid a fight by leaving, and their spouse blocks the door, preventing their escape. One person I've counseled was chased by his spouse all around the yard before he finally pushed her to the ground. The police charged him with domestic violence, and he spent a week in jail. I told him that it was the best thing that could have happened to him because now he understood why he had to learn to control his temper under the most irritating conditions. If he didn't, he would spend even more time in jail the next time he failed.

Relaxation in the face of terribly irritating conditions reverses the physiological cause of an angry outburst—adrenaline. When you are faced with a threat, adrenaline is secreted, and it builds up in your blood, affecting the way your brain operates. It triggers neural pathways that lead to irrational thoughts, and you are motivated to behave with vengeance. If you don't calm down when faced with adversity, you cannot think rationally when you need your intelligence the most. Your intuitive response is to lash out at the one causing your frustration. And when that person is your spouse, you can't let that happen.

So I trained Sam to relax when in frustrating situations. While using biofeedback equipment to measure his emotional reactions, we discussed some of the most annoying experiences he had ever faced. After measurements indicated that he was agitated, I asked him to relax all of his muscles, going from the top of his head to the bottom of his feet. As he learned to voluntarily relax his muscles when he began feeling tense, he was able to reduce the time it would take to calm himself down. I sent him home with a device that gave him feedback regarding his emotional state, so he could practice relaxing throughout the week.

You can practice relaxing under adversity without using biofeedback equipment. All that's needed is your ability to imagine something your spouse does that frustrates you, and then to relax after you think about it. Instead of feeling increasingly resentful about the situation, you will find yourself feeling more objective. You will be able to think about solutions to the problem instead of becoming angry.

Quite frankly, anger management training takes time, because it's not just the adrenaline you are learning to reduce. It's also the neural pathways that you are changing. By responding to adversity with relaxation, you are training your brain to think rationally when faced with frustrating situations, instead of responding to them with anger. The more you practice calming down when frustrated, the more your brain changes the way it handles those situations. After a while, you don't even feel angry when annoyed. Instead, you think about the problem in an intelligent and rational way.

Years ago, some therapists felt that the way to deal with anger was to express it openly. Punching bags were given to clients to vent their frustrations. Based on my own analysis of the problem, you would expect that these methods would have made matters worse—and they did. By venting your anger, you are reinforcing the neural pathways that cause you to respond to frustration with an angry outburst. Today, there are very few who use that technique because it doesn't work. On the other hand, most specialists in anger management have come to recognize the value of relaxation techniques in helping people eliminate angry outbursts. And they also notice that the longer these people apply these techniques, the less angry they feel. Their brains are actually changing to make them wise when they feel that they're under attack.

Angry outbursts in marriage should be avoided at all costs, because they represent an extreme form of abuse. And mistakes made by the other spouse should never be viewed as an excuse. This means that when you feel irritated, instead of venting your anger, you walk away. If you can't walk away, you learn how to relax. In some cases, you may need to separate from your spouse to avoid being abused yourself. But under no circumstances should you ever allow yourself to become the abuser.

The goal of an effective program of anger management is to avoid an angry outburst when you're irritated the most, when people seem the most insensitive. If you can't achieve that objective on your own by following my plan to overcome angry outbursts, find a therapist who has a proven record in helping spouses avoid domestic violence. The therapist you choose should not only teach spouses to avoid angry outbursts, but he or she should also be able to keep the marriage together during therapy. Be careful to avoid therapists who try to solve your anger problem by encouraging you to end your marriage.

### Step 6: Measure your progress.

With Sam and Jill both present in my office, I handed her a form with these instructions:

*Please list all instances of your spouse's angry outbursts and acts that you consider punishment for something you did. These include verbal and physical acts of anger and threatened acts of anger toward you, cursing you, and making disrespectful or belittling comments about you. Include the day, date, time, and circumstances, along with a description of each angry outburst.*

I asked Jill to keep a record of how well Sam kept his commitment to control his temper. Measuring progress is a crucial step in this plan to overcome angry outbursts, and the victim is usually the best one to do the measuring. Jill, more than anyone else, would know when Sam slipped up. As I mentioned earlier, we tend to forget what we did when we're angry, so those who have difficulty controlling their anger are not qualified to measure their own progress. Furthermore, Jill's documentation would be a big help in understanding precisely what it was that she would consider an angry outburst. I told her that a simple raising of Sam's voice when he was frustrated could make it to her list if she felt that it was an expression of anger.

Before they left my office, I told Sam that he would have to accept as truth whatever Jill wrote down. He was not to argue with her about her interpretation of his behavior, but just try to avoid doing it in the future. I warned him that there would be some surprises the first week.

Sure enough, when they had their next appointment, only three days later, she had already written down two instances of angry outbursts—and one of them was in the parking lot on the way out of my office.

"Why is she doing this to me?" Sam complained. "I didn't lose my temper. All I did was tell her that I didn't think we needed to go through all of this. Can't I express my feelings anymore?"

I explained that this was one of the surprises I had warned Sam about. It was important for him to understand exactly how Jill interpreted his "expression of feelings." To her it was punishment. I suggested that he should not express his frustration to her until he felt very relaxed.

Two days later, I talked to him again on the telephone, and he proudly announced that Jill had no new entries since my last appointment with him. For the first time he realized that his expression of frustration when agitated threatened Jill and made her unhappy. He would need to learn how to talk to her when he was relaxed, so that she would feel safe.

When I saw Jill and Sam for their next appointment, I talked with her first and read the entries in her progress report. She explained how difficult it had been to be truthful, because she was afraid that the report itself would cause Sam to lose his temper. It's true. Some of my clients have reacted to the report with angry outbursts. One man actually tore it up when he read it because he did not agree with his wife's report.

Whenever that happens, it brings into focus the seriousness of the spouse's problem. In some cases a more intense plan of action must be created to address the fact that the anger is out of control. And, as I already mentioned, I have encouraged many couples to separate until a spouse can prove enough control to guarantee the other spouse's safety.

If you are trying to overcome angry outbursts, ask your spouse to measure your progress, just as Jill measured Sam's progress. As was also the case with selfish demands and disrespectful judgments, your spouse is the best judge of your behavior.

At this point you might ask the question, how long should my spouse go on documenting any instances of my angry outbursts? My answer: for the rest of your life. Of course if you're successful there won't be any instances to document. But if you ever do something in the future that your spouse interprets as an angry outburst, he or she should have the right to bring it to your attention and you should have the responsibility of acknowledging it, apologizing for it, and analyzing what went wrong. Did you follow the plan? Is there a new condition that makes

Love Busters

it particularly difficult to control your temper? Whenever you have an angry outburst, you should address the issue immediately so that you can avoid it in the future.

## Controlling Your Temper Can Save Your Marriage

After following these steps, Sam completely eliminated his verbal abuse and even his feelings of anger toward Jill. He explained some of the changes in his thinking to me.

"I know what makes me feel angry. It is thinking that Jill doesn't really care about me and that all she cares about is herself. But if I relax, I stop thinking those thoughts, and I tell myself that we will be able to work out our problems."

Jill really did care about Sam and wanted to have a family with him someday. She was definitely on his side and wanted him to succeed in controlling his anger. Within a few weeks, they were engaged in serious negotiations about the way her work affected him, and she made some very important changes to accommodate his feelings, particularly about the way she talked to him about her boss. She also made a point of avoiding any contact with her boss that was not purely business-related.

Sam's anger had driven her away from him, and now that he had proven that he could protect her from it, she was drawn back to him, something he had wanted all along.

They also came to some very important agreements regarding child-rearing techniques. I warned them that Sam's tendency toward anger could easily be resurrected once their children arrived, and that would also make withdrawals from Jill's Love Bank. So they both agreed that any discipline would be mutually and *enthusiastically* agreed to, or it wouldn't happen. And if he were ever angry toward their children, he would do nothing to punish them. Instead, he would relax.

People who have not learned to control their anger are far more likely to have bad marriages and, ultimately, to divorce. But if you can recognize anger for what it really is, a Love Buster, and learn how to protect your spouse from it, you will not only save your marriage but

110

you will also save yourself from a life of endless searching for someone who will put up with your anger.

Despite what some have thought in the past, controlling your anger does not cause you to build resentment, and does not lead to serious emotional problems. I've counseled hundreds of people who have been successful in protecting their spouse from their angry outbursts, and none of them became more resentful or went crazy. Instead, they felt a lot better about themselves, and their spouses felt downright emancipated. It made finding solutions to their problems much easier to do.

As I've said repeatedly, anger should have no place in marriage. It should not be tolerated. While it is a normal human reaction, it is also a destructive reaction, and you must protect your spouse from it if your spouse is to be happy and secure living with you.

> *If you can recognize anger for what it really is, a Love Buster, and learn how to protect your spouse from it, you will not only save your marriage but you will also save yourself from a life of endless searching for someone who will put up with your anger.*

Selfish demands, disrespectful judgments, and angry outbursts very often blend into each other. Sometimes it's a little difficult to know what is a selfish demand, what is a disrespectful judgment, and what is an angry outburst, because in many arguments you have them all at once. When a spouse is making a demand he might also be disrespectful and angry at the same time. That's one of the reasons that I put these three Love Busters on a continuum of control and abuse. All three of them represent ways that you try to get what you need by taking advantage of your spouse.

These three Love Busters are all very instinctive and can be seen in most of us when we're just a year old. Demands, disrespect, and anger are strategies that we're all born with to get our way. But just as they're inappropriate for children and we try to teach children to avoid them, they're certainly inappropriate in marriage. If your parents didn't do a very good job teaching you to avoid demands, disrespect, and anger, for the sake of your marriage and your spouse, you need to learn to avoid them now. And you can learn to avoid them.

Marriages turn completely around when spouses have decided not to tolerate their own anger, disrespect, and demands. It gives them the opportunity to negotiate effectively. That's how you and your spouse can really get what you need from each other. And I want you to have what you need in your marriage.

But if your marriage is infected by selfish demands, disrespectful judgments, and angry outbursts, you will not be able to give each other what you need. Instead, you will grow in incompatibility. It's only by eliminating these Love Busters that you give your intelligence a chance to make the wise choices that take the interests of both of you into account. By doing that, you'll both be making deposits into each other's Love Banks simultaneously.

## Key Principles

My plan to help you overcome angry outbursts consists of six steps:

Step 1  Acknowledge the fact that you, and only you, determine if you will have an angry outburst. No one "makes" you angry.

Step 2  Identify instances of your angry outbursts and their effects.

Step 3  Understand why your angry outbursts take place.

Step 4  Try to avoid the conditions that make angry outbursts difficult to control.

Step 5  Train yourself to control your temper when you cannot avoid frustrating situations.

Step 6  Measure your progress.

If my plan to help you overcome your outbursts doesn't work for you when you try it on your own, seek professional help to guarantee your spouse's safety. You should have zero tolerance for your angry outbursts.

## Consider This . . . ———————————

1. Do you take full responsibility for your angry outbursts, or do you blame them on your spouse? Remember, you will not be able to overcome your angry outbursts until you realize that you, and only you, can control them.

2. If you are in the habit of having angry outbursts when you have a conflict, it will take practice to avoid them. Agree with each other that if either of you feels angry during a discussion, you will break off your conversation and relax. Let adrenaline dissipate from your system before you return to the topic.

3. If either of you cannot seem to gain control over your angry outbursts, I suggest you find professional help. Most hospitals and mental health clinics offer anger management therapy that has proven to be effective. But not all therapy is equal, so be certain that the therapist you select is recommended by doctors or social service agencies who have witnessed firsthand their effectiveness in treating this serious problem. And also be certain that they follow the six steps in my plan to overcome angry outbursts.

# 10

## Dishonesty: *Part 1*

### Who Wants to Live with a Liar?

The first time Jennifer was dishonest with Ed about her feelings was during their honeymoon. They were having dinner together in a restaurant that was on the beach. The evening was beautiful, and from where they were seated, they could watch the waves crashing onto the sand.

Then Ed's cell phone rang, and the mood suddenly changed. Ed had given his number to some of his best customers and one of them wanted help with a problem.

Ed excused himself to talk to his customer, leaving Jennifer to enjoy the scenery and her dinner—alone. Half an hour later Ed returned, with apologies for the interruption.

Though Jennifer was deeply offended by the way Ed had treated her, she did not tell him how bad she felt. Instead, she told him how much she was enjoying the scenery.

That call at dinner was not the only one that interrupted their honeymoon. Ed received several calls, even one while he and Jennifer were about to make love. Jennifer was hurt that Ed was trying to conduct business during their honeymoon, but she never let him know. She wanted him to be successful in his business and felt she had to learn to adjust.

While they had been dating, Jennifer found it easy to be honest with Ed about her feelings. He was a great guy, always trying to make her happy, so her accolades far outweighed her complaints. On the few occasions when he did something that upset her, she mentioned it briefly, and he quickly made accommodations. But after they were married, she didn't feel that it was appropriate for her to let him know when she was offended, because it was almost always job-related. For example, he left her home alone three nights each week, which bothered her. But she let him think she was happy with the arrangement. She knew how important his demanding job was for both of them.

By the time they had children, both Ed and Jennifer had become increasingly preoccupied with the ever-escalating responsibilities of life. Their marriage suffered because they neglected each other's emotional needs, but neither Ed nor Jennifer thought it was right to complain. In fact, they had read a marriage book that warned them to avoid complaining. Their dishonesty was now mutual and growing.

Ed felt unfulfilled with their sexual relationship, but he understood the pressure Jennifer was under. After a long day of child care, he knew she'd be tired when he came home from work late at night. He felt that it would be unfair to expect her to meet his sexual needs whenever he felt amorous. So he didn't tell her about his increasing sexual frustration.

Jennifer was also growing increasingly frustrated with Ed's neglect of her. Once in a great while, when he came home after another late night at the office, she'd admit, "I'm feeling lonely."

Ed would react with a sigh of resignation, "It took me longer than I thought to close the sale. I'll try to be home earlier next time, but I can't hurry these things along."

"Yeah, I guess you're right." Jennifer would drop the subject and Ed would think she was satisfied with his answer. But she wasn't. She had told him how she felt, and he didn't seem to care.

And Ed even told Jennifer how he felt about their sexual relationship—once. When Jennifer explained that the children made her feel too tired at night, he said he understood. And he did, but the problem still bothered him.

Meanwhile, both Ed and Jennifer were innocently creating incompatibility. Slowly but surely they were growing apart because neither one said anything when his or her emotional needs were not met. Eventually, they were no longer in love with each other.

### Why Is Dishonesty a Love Buster?

As you've seen in the opening example, dishonesty helps create incompatibility in marriage. Information that is essential to a couple's adjustment to each other is not made available. Without that information, a couple fails to meet each other's emotional needs and grows apart.

Another reason that dishonesty cripples marriages is that honesty is one of the most important emotional needs in marriage, especially for women. Dishonesty in any form prevents a spouse from meeting that need. When a spouse has been lied to, they don't know what to believe. One lie makes almost all other statements suspect.

But the primary reason that I consider dishonesty to be a Love Buster is because, when discovered, it causes massive Love Bank withdrawals. Most spouses, especially wives, find dishonesty to be intolerable. Even little white lies rock the very foundation of a couple's love for each other. Most spouses can't imagine living with a liar.

And yet, as is true for all of the other Love Busters I introduce in this book, dishonesty is common in marriage. What's also true is that it's difficult to root it out. How can you know for sure that your spouse is being honest with you, especially when he or she has been dishonest in the past? Armed with a careful analysis of this problem presented in this chapter, and a proven path to changing dishonesty into honesty in the next chapter, you should be able to come away with hope for change in your marriage that you may not have experienced before.

### Types of Dishonesty

There are four types of dishonesty in marriage: (1) protection, (2) looking good, (3) avoiding trouble, and (4) compulsion. While the motives and excuses are very different for each type, the result is the same—the marriage suffers.

### Protector Liars

Ed and Jennifer were making a common mistake. In an effort to protect each other from unpleasant information, they were failing to be honest about their reactions to each other's behavior. Love Bank withdrawals were tumbling out of their Love Bank accounts without a word being said.

In most marriages, people tend to keep a certain amount of negative feedback from each other because they don't want to appear to be nagging or complaining too much. Almost everybody can think of times when they have withheld their true feelings or unpleasant information to avoid upsetting their spouse. But whenever that happens, they become "protector liars."

> *The problem with protective lying is that it does not protect— it denies a spouse crucial information.*

It seems quite innocent, doesn't it? But the problem with protective lying is that it does not protect—it *denies* a spouse crucial information. As Ed and Jennifer "protected" each other from the truth about their feelings, they were becoming increasingly incompatible and they were losing their love for each other. Ed's work schedule was siphoning love units out of Jennifer's Love Bank, but she didn't let him know how it was affecting her. Each time Jennifer turned down Ed's sexual advances, she was making withdrawals in Ed's Love Bank, but he pretended that there was nothing wrong.

How would you feel if your bank stopped giving you monthly statements on your checking account but continued to deduct fees for overdrafts without informing you? You'd be outraged. "When our customers run out of money in their accounts," the bank manager might say, "we try to protect them from that unpleasant information." That's crazy! You need accurate information the most when you're overdrawn, so you can deposit enough to avoid bouncing checks.

The same is true in marriage. If Jennifer and Ed had known how often they were making Love Bank withdrawals, they could have made adjustments to prevent further losses. But without that information, they were blindly drifting out of love.

### Trying-to-Look-Better-Than-You-Are Liars

It would be bad enough if lying to protect were the only type of dishonesty to infect marriage. But dishonesty in marriage can take several forms, and Steve, as you'll see below, suffered from a second type of dishonesty in his marriage to Sally—lying to look better than he was.

Some people need admiration and approval so much that they try to make themselves look better than they really are. To leave a favorable impression, these liars fabricate achievements and abilities so that others will have higher regard for them. Most of us want to put our best foot forward, but this type of liar misrepresents the facts. For some, it's just an embellishment of something that actually took place, but for others, the entire event is a lie.

Steve was a trying-to-look-better-than-he-was liar. It started when he first dated Sally. He knew that she had done well in school, so he made up stories about his school achievements. As far as she knew, he was among the top in his class. But the truth was that he was an underachiever. Granted, he had the ability to get good grades, but he never really gave it much effort. Those A's and B's that he told her he earned were actually C's and D's. He hardly made it through high school, but who ever checks school records?

Then, during their marriage, Steve continued to exaggerate his achievements, especially those at work. When Sally asked him how his day went, he often made up stories about sales he made and commendations he received from his supervisor. She would tell him how proud she was of him, and to keep up the good work.

His stories were so convincing that he believed some of them himself. On one occasion when he was asking for a raise, he reminded his supervisor of an outstanding sale he had recently made, only to remember halfway through the conversation that it was merely one of the stories he had told his wife. It was embarrassing when he had to admit it never happened, but he got out of the situation by blaming his poor memory and dropping his request for a raise.

But Steve knew it was not really a memory problem—it was an honesty problem. He had developed the habit of lying to make himself look better than he really was. He thought he could keep up the deception throughout his marriage, but lies have a way of tripping us up eventually.

### Avoid-Trouble Liars

Dishonesty can spread like a virus. One lie can lead to another, and one type of lying can lead to another type of lying. Steve's lying to look good created problems for him that led to yet a third type of dishonesty—lying to avoid trouble. It arises from the threat of being caught doing something wrong.

What is right and wrong, of course, is often in the eyes of the beholder, so "avoid-trouble liars" often feel that their own shady actions are appropriate but they suspect that others will judge them harshly if they were to know the truth. In marriage, these people do things that their spouse would disapprove of, but to avoid their spouse's judgment, they lie.

Sally suspected that Steve was embellishing his sales record, and so one day she mustered up the courage to call his supervisor to get the facts. After he explained that he was not authorized to reveal personal information about employees, she didn't give up. She went on to ask where she could find information on her husband's sales records. After telling her that he was not authorized to reveal any information about Steve, he suggested that she speak to their personnel department. That call left her devastated. They told her that he had been released six weeks earlier for poor performance.

Steve had not only been lying to her about having an outstanding sales record, but he had been fired six weeks earlier. He had been warned several times that if his sales did not improve they could not continue to employ him, and they finally had let him go.

For six weeks, Steve had left the house each day pretending to go to work. But instead of going to his old job he was looking for a new one. He had hoped to find something quickly and tell Sally that he quit the old job for a better offer, so that she would be none the wiser.

Was Steve's lie to Sally to make himself look better than he was, or was it to avoid trouble? Sometimes a lie has many motives, and in this case, there could be an argument made for a little of both. But when Steve pretended to go to work, he was definitely trying to avoid trouble. If he were to tell Sally he had been fired, his lies about his sales would unravel and he would be seen as the underachiever he really was.

But Sally was not innocent when it came to dishonesty. She also suffered from the ravages of avoid-trouble lying. Always short of cash, she hated begging Steve for money. So she opened her own bank account by forging her husband's signature on a ten-thousand-dollar loan application. She planned to make the payments with the money she earned working part-time. Steve suspected that something was going on, because she seemed to have an expensive new outfit just about every week. But she claimed that she was simply finding incredible bargains.

Sally's plan might have gone undetected if she hadn't lost her part-time job, and then missed a payment on the loan. When Steve got a call from the bank, the cat was out of the bag.

"None of this would have happened if Steve hadn't been so cheap" was Sally's excuse. According to her, she had a right to spend more money than Steve gave her, and so she took matters into her own hands. She justified her dishonesty as necessary for her survival.

People who have affairs often feel the same way about their behavior. With their spouse unwilling to meet their needs, they are "forced," they claim, to find another who is willing. Most people caught in affairs are more upset about the fact that they were caught than they are about the pain they've caused their spouse and children. They are outraged by their spouse's snooping—invading their privacy. While admitting that they hurt their spouse, remarkably few actually feel guilty about it. They tend to believe that if their spouse had met their needs in the first place, they would not have had to go to the trouble of finding someone else.

Lying is bad enough, but trying to shift blame to the offended spouse is adding insult to injury. A humble and contrite apology is the only appropriate response to an uncovered lie. But most liars make matters worse by trying to defend their indefensible act.

## Compulsive Liars

I call those who lie about anything and everything, whether they have a good reason to lie or not, "compulsive liars," because they don't seem to be able to control it, nor do they know why they do it. These people often lie about trivial experiences and don't seem to know what is true and what is not. Even solid evidence to the contrary does not always dissuade them.

Compulsive liars sometimes live double lives. Occasionally you'll read a news story about a con artist who has finally been caught after passing himself off as a doctor or lawyer, or marrying two or more people. These people are usually compulsive liars. When caught red-handed in a crime, they sincerely deny any involvement and can even pass lie detector tests. Such liars are fascinating to psychologists such as me, but for obvious reasons they're impossible as marriage partners. Since honesty is essential in marriage, and these individuals simply cannot tell the truth, their marriages are usually very short-lived.

This fourth category, compulsive lying, is the most extreme form of dishonesty and the most difficult to treat in therapy. Thankfully, very few of the spouses I counsel have this affliction. Since this form of lying should be quite obvious to anyone with an inquisitive mind early on, compulsive liars usually do not get very far in romantic relationships. Those who end up marrying such people usually have so little interest in their personal lives that they miss the obvious red flags. It's rare for anyone to be that disinterested.

If you and your spouse struggle with dishonesty, chances are that it falls into the categories of lying to protect, to look good, or to avoid trouble. I've found that these liars can overcome this Love Buster by practicing the kind of honesty that I will describe to you in the next chapter.

## Can Honesty Be a Love Buster?

As you contemplate what your marriage might be like if you were honest with each other, you may be wondering if honesty, in some cases, is a Love Buster itself. Are there times when a couple can be *too* honest with each other, and when it would be better to avoid conflict by keeping a spouse in the dark?

That's what Ed and Jennifer believed. They assumed their relationship would suffer harm if they expressed their true feelings. And on the surface, this argument seems to make sense. Love Busters are habits that make your spouse unhappy; so if your expression of honesty troubles your spouse, it must be a Love Buster, right?

But if you take a closer look, you find that the Love Buster usually isn't the honesty itself, but the behavior that honesty reveals. Confessing to an affair will certainly upset your spouse, but it isn't the confession that's upsetting. It's the affair! In fact, lying about it makes it even more upsetting.

Dishonesty usually only postpones your spouse's discovery of the truth, and once it's revealed, your spouse will be upset by both your thoughtless behavior and your dishonesty. And of the two, your dishonesty will usually hurt your spouse more than whatever it was you were trying to conceal. Dishonesty in marriage, once discovered, causes incredible pain. That's why it's dishonesty—not honesty—that is a Love Buster.

### Don't Wrap Your Honesty in Love Busters

While we are on the subject of how the disclosure of truth can be painful, couples often make it much more painful than it needs to be. That's because disclosure of truth can be accompanied by Love Busters.

In reaction to Ed's failure to be home with Jennifer in the evenings, suppose she had greeted him at the door with, "You never have time for me anymore, you selfish jerk! I don't know why I ever married you!" She gets points for honesty, but her disrespectful judgment and angry outburst ruin it all. Ed would not hear her complaint about his neglect because he'd be running for cover.

Or suppose that Ed were to decide to take the same approach to his sexual frustration as Jim did in my opening illustration—by demanding sex. That's one way to get your feelings out on the table, but it's honesty wrapped in demands. And it would communicate brutal selfishness to Jennifer, not an unmet emotional need.

*In conquering the Love Buster of dishonesty, you must do more than reveal the truth. You must make sure you express it in a way that informs without needlessly causing harm.*

Many people wrap their honest feelings in the poison of Love Busters. When they try to express their complaints with selfish demands, disrespectful judgments, and angry outbursts, havoc results and so they go back to bottling up their feelings. They think, *I tried being honest and look where it got me.*

It's not easy to express honest feelings without being demanding, disrespectful, or angry, but if you don't avoid those Love Busters, you will fail to communicate your needs to each other effectively. Here are two examples of how to be honest without being abusive:

- "I'm the least important person in your life; you'd rather be with anyone else but me," is a disrespectful judgment because you are making a sweeping generalization about your spouse's priorities and opinions. A less judgmental statement might be, "I know that you're uncomfortable being with me right now." But even that's a bad idea, since you are *telling* your spouse how he or she feels. In contrast, "I become upset when I'm left alone at night" is an honest expression with no Love Busters in sight, because you are merely explaining to your spouse how *you* feel.

- "If you don't start spending more time with me soon, I'll find someone else to join me in the evenings," is a selfish demand. It comes with a threat of punishment if you don't obey. "I'd like to spend more time with you" is an honest way to communicate your feelings without using Love Busters.

In conquering the Love Buster of dishonesty, you must do more than reveal the truth. You must make sure you express it in a way that informs without needlessly causing harm.

## Discouraging Honesty with Your Values and Reactions

You may want your spouse to be honest, but do your own values discourage it? And do your reactions discourage your spouse from revealing the truth? To see how you rate, answer these questions:

1. If the truth is terribly upsetting to you, do you want your spouse to be honest only at a time when you are emotionally prepared?
2. Do you keep some aspects of your life secret and do you encourage your spouse to respect your privacy in those areas?
3. Do you have well-defined boundaries that you encourage your spouse not to cross?
4. Do you like to create a certain mystery between you and your spouse?
5. Are there subjects or situations where you would want to avoid honesty?
6. Do you ever make selfish demands when your spouse is honest with you?
7. Do you ever make disrespectful judgments when your spouse is honest with you?
8. Do you ever have angry outbursts when your spouse is honest with you?

If you answer "yes" to any of the first five questions, you tend to compromise on the value of honesty. Apparently you feel your marriage is better off with dishonesty in certain situations. That little crack is all dishonesty needs to slip into your marriage and run amok. You see, there are always "reasons" to be dishonest. As soon as you allow one to sneak in, it will invite all its friends, and before you know it, you have a dishonest relationship.

If you answered "yes" to questions 6, 7, or 8, you are punishing honesty and encouraging dishonesty. The way to help your spouse learn to be truthful is to minimize the negative consequences of his or her truthful revelations. If your spouse is faced with a fight whenever truth is revealed, you invite dishonesty. Your spouse will learn to say anything to avoid arguing—and then do what he or she pleases. But what if there are no fights? No judgments? No demands? If you can eliminate these Love Busters, you'll make it much easier for your spouse to be honest with you.

Once you've been able to overcome dishonesty, you'll find your relationship improving in many different ways. You will have not only eliminated this great offense to your spouse, but by being honest you'll have opened the door to effective ways to resolve conflicts. Radical honesty will give you a much clearer understanding of both the conflict itself and how each of you will react to possible resolutions. By having the facts on the table, it will be much easier to find solutions that make you happy simultaneously.

Without the barrier of unspoken opinions, beliefs, and feelings, you'll be able to cut to the chase, understand each other quickly, protect each other's feelings, and create solutions to your conflicts that will help you build a deeper love for each other. And that's my ultimate goal for your marriage. I want you to be in love. And the way for you to be in love is to make each other happy by meeting each other's important emotional needs, and avoid making each other unhappy by eliminating Love Busters such as dishonesty.

## Key Principles

There are four types of dishonesty in marriage: (1) protection, (2) trying to look better than you are, (3) avoiding trouble, and (4) compulsion.

Honesty is not a Love Buster. When thoughtless behavior is revealed, it's the thoughtless behavior, not the honesty that causes unhappiness.

Avoid wrapping honesty in the Love Busters of selfish demands, disrespectful judgments, or angry outbursts.

Encourage your spouse to be honest by valuing honesty, and by avoiding its punishment.

## Consider This . . .

1. Is dishonesty a problem in your marriage? To answer that question, complete the dishonesty page (page 215) of the Love Busters

Questionnaire in Appendix B. Make two enlarged copies, one for each of you, so that you will have enough space to write your answers.

2. How important is it for your spouse to be honest with you? Are there situations where you would encourage your spouse to be dishonest? If the truth is terribly upsetting to you, do you want your spouse to be honest only at a time when you are emotionally prepared? Do you keep some aspects of your life secret and do you encourage your spouse to respect your privacy in those areas?

3. Do you reward honesty, or do you punish it? Do you ever have angry outbursts, make disrespectful judgments, or make selfish demands when your spouse is honest with you?

# 11

Dishonesty: *Part 2*

## How to Turn Dishonesty
## into Radical Honesty

In chapter 5, I introduced you to a rule that will help you resolve conflicts the right way—with win-win outcomes. It's the Policy of Joint Agreement: *Never do anything without an enthusiastic agreement between you and your spouse.* This rule reminds both of you that almost everything you do affects each other with either Love Bank deposits or withdrawals. So if you want to be in love with each other, your conflicts should be resolved in a way that makes deposits into both of your Love Banks, and not just one of them.

But if your decisions are to be effective in making Love Bank deposits, they require more than just enthusiastic agreement. They also require honesty from both spouses. If some of the facts, opinions, or feelings are hidden, a successful win-win outcome usually can't be found.

So I've added a second rule for couples to follow to help them overcome this problem. I call it the **Policy of Radical Honesty:** *Reveal to your spouse as much information about yourself as you know—your thoughts, feelings, likes, dislikes, past history, daily activities, and plans for the future.*

This rule is as important for marriage as the Policy of Joint Agreement, because without it, an agreement wouldn't necessarily solve a problem. But it does much more for a marriage than just support the Policy of Joint Agreement. It also helps lead spouses to the wisest and most mutually advantageous decisions.

## Policy of Radical Honesty

*Reveal to your spouse as much information about yourself as you know—your thoughts, feelings, likes, dislikes, past history, daily activities, and plans for the future.*

And if that were not enough, radical honesty also meets a very important emotional need, especially for women. Couples that fail to be radically honest with each other have little hope of ever having a fulfilling marriage.

But the third reason to be radically honest in marriage is the focus of this chapter: dishonesty is a Love Buster that, when discovered, makes massive Love Bank withdrawals. It destroys the trust you need for a fulfilling marriage and should not be tolerated. The habit of radical honesty should replace the habit of dishonesty.

Why do I call this policy "radical" ? It's because many feel that a little dishonesty here and there is normal and to be expected. We are all witnesses to the lies and deceit practiced by many of our leaders in business, politics, and even the clergy. It's easy to come away with the impression that honesty is optional in life, and should be applied only when convenient. So when I advocate complete honesty in marriage, many feel that my advice is radical. Instead of dodging the issue, I celebrate it. Honesty *is* radical. And yet, if you want a great marriage, it's essential.

To eliminate any confusion as to how honest I encourage spouses to be with each other, I'll focus attention on each of the four parts of the Policy of Radical Honesty:

1. *Emotional Honesty:* Reveal your thoughts, feelings, likes, and dislikes. In other words, reveal your emotional reactions—both positive and negative—to the events of your life, particularly to your spouse's behavior.

2. *Historical Honesty:* Reveal information about your personal history, particularly events that demonstrate personal weakness or failure.

3. *Current Honesty:* Reveal information about the events of your day. Provide your spouse with a calendar of your activities, with special emphasis on those that may affect your spouse.

4. *Future Honesty:* Reveal your thoughts and plans regarding future activities and objectives.

## Emotional Honesty

Most couples do their best to make each other happy, at least at first. But their efforts, however sincere, are often misdirected. They aim at the wrong target.

Emotional honesty enables a couple to make appropriate adjustments to each other. And adjustment is what a good marriage is all about. Both of you are growing and changing almost daily and you must constantly adjust to each other's changes if you are to remain compatible. But how can you know how to adjust if you're not receiving accurate information about these changes? You'd be flying blind, like a pilot without an instrument panel.

Some people find it difficult to express their emotional reactions, particularly the negative ones. But negative feelings serve a valuable purpose in a marriage. They are a signal that something is wrong. If you successfully steer clear of the three Love Busters, selfish demands, disrespectful judgments, and angry outbursts, your expression of negative feelings can alert both you and your spouse to an adjustment that should be made.

In addition to expressing negative emotions honestly, don't overlook the expression of positive feelings. These are generally easier to communicate, yet many couples have not learned to communicate them well. And by this failure, they miss an important opportunity to *deposit* love units. Whenever your spouse makes *you* feel good, if you express those feelings clearly and enthusiastically, you'll make *your spouse* feel good, knowing that his or her care is appreciated.

The mere communication of feelings does not assure that all the necessary adjustments will be made. There is still work to do. But without honest communication, failure is guaranteed.

### Historical Honesty

Should your skeletons stay in the closet?

Some say yes: Lock the door, hide the key, and leave well enough alone. Communicate your past misdeeds only on a need-to-know basis.

But your spouse always needs to know. Whatever embarrassing experiences or serious mistakes are in your past, you should come clean with your spouse in the present.

Your personal history holds significant information about you—information about your strengths and weaknesses. Your spouse needs to understand both your good and bad points if appropriate adjustments are to be made.

A man who has had an affair in the past is particularly vulnerable to another one. If a woman has been chemically dependent in the past, she'll be susceptible to drug or alcohol abuse in the future. If you express your past mistakes openly, your spouse can understand your weaknesses, and together you can avoid conditions that tend to create problems for you.

No area of your life should be kept secret. All questions asked by your spouse should be answered fully and completely. Periods of poor adjustment in your past should be given special attention, because problems of the past are commonly problems of the future.

I also encourage you to reveal to each other all romantic relationships you've had in the past. Names should be included along with a description of what happened.

"But if I tell my wife what I've done, she'll never trust me again."

"If my husband finds out about my past, he'll be crushed. It will ruin his whole image of me."

I have heard these protests from various clients trying to hide their past. *Why dig it all up?* they ask. *Let that old affair stay buried in ancient history. Why not just leave that little demon alone?* I answer that it's not a little demon but an extremely important part of their personal story that says something about their habits and character.

But what if you haven't strayed since it happened? What if you've seen a pastor regularly to hold you accountable? Why put your spouse through the agony of a revelation that could ruin your relationship forever?

If that's your argument, I'd say you don't give your spouse much credit. Honesty doesn't drive a spouse away—*dishonesty* does. When you hold something back, your spouse tries to guess what it is. If he or she is correct, then you must continually lie to cover your tracks. If incorrect, your spouse develops a false understanding of you and your predispositions.

Maybe you don't really want to be known for who you are. That's sad, isn't it? You'd rather keep your secret than experience one of life's greatest joys—to be loved and accepted in spite of known weaknesses.

While revealing your past will strengthen your marriage, it's not necessarily painless. Some spouses have difficulty adjusting to revelations that have been kept secret for years—the saints they thought they married turn out to be mere mortals. To control the emotional damage of particularly shocking revelations, it may be helpful to express them to your spouse in the presence of a professional counselor. Some spouses may need some personal support to help them adjust to the reality of their spouse's past.

In cases I've witnessed, however, spouses tend to react more negatively to the long-term deception than to the concealed event. The thoughtless act might be accepted and forgiven, but the cover-up is often harder to understand. If you reveal it instead of waiting for your spouse to discover it, though, it's proof that you are taking honesty in your marriage seriously and will be making an effort in the future to avoid the Love Buster of dishonesty.

You may find historical honesty to be frightening, and that's understandable. But let me assure you that I've never seen a marriage destroyed by truth. When truth is revealed, there are often negative reactions and some shaky times, but ultimately the truth makes marriages stronger.

## Current Honesty

In good marriages couples become so interdependent that sharing a daily schedule is essential to their coordination of activities. But in weak marriages they are reluctant to reveal their schedules because they often engage in activities that they want to keep from their spouse. They hide the details of their day, telling themselves, "What he doesn't know won't hurt him," or "She's happier not knowing everything."

Even when activities are innocent, it's extremely important for your spouse to understand what you do with your time. Make sure you're easy to find in an emergency or when your spouse just wants to say hello during the day. Keep your cell phones close by so that contact is possible 24/7. Almost everything you do will affect each other, so it's important to know what each of you is doing.

Current honesty is a terrific way to protect your spouse from potentially damaging predispositions and inappropriate activities. When you know that you'll be telling your spouse what you've been up to, you're far less likely to do anything that would get you into trouble.

## Future Honesty

After I've made such a big issue of revealing past indiscretions, you can imagine how I feel about revealing future plans. They're *much* easier to discuss with your spouse, yet many couples make plans independently of each other. Why?

Some people believe that communicating future plans just gives a spouse the opportunity to quash them. They have their sights set on a certain goal and they don't want anything to stand in their way. You may be trying to avoid trouble in the present, but eventually the future will arrive and your plans will be revealed. At that point your spouse will be hurt that you didn't consider their feelings when you made your plans. And that will withdraw love units.

The Policy of Joint Agreement—*Never do anything without an enthusiastic agreement between you and your spouse*—is certainly relevant in discussions of your future plans.

"If I wait for my wife to agree," a husband might say, "we'll never accomplish anything. She's so conservative, she never wants to take any risks, and so we miss every opportunity that comes along." But isn't that approach, in essence, a disrespectful judgment, forcing the husband's perspective onto the wife? If he genuinely cares about her, he will want to include her interests and feelings in every decision.

"Oh, but the plans I make are best for both of us," a wife might say. "He may not understand my decision now but once he sees how things turn out, he'll thank me for going ahead with it." That's disrespectful. Even if your plans work out, your spouse will still feel offended about not being included in the planning.

### Learning to Be in the Habit of Radical Honesty

In the following section, I go into quite a bit of detail regarding my recommended preparation, execution, and evaluation of your plan to overcome dishonesty. I do this because success in eliminating this Love Buster is usually very difficult to achieve, even for seasoned therapists. Many have never had any training in helping dishonest clients, let alone experience in successfully teaching them to become honest.

But I have had that experience, and what I've learned is that careful preparation, execution, and evaluation of a plan to overcome dishonesty is essential to your success. So bear with me as I lay out a procedure that I've followed for many years that provides the best outcome I've ever witnessed.

### *Step 1: Why are you dishonest?*

First, you should understand how and why dishonesty has established itself in your marriage. You achieve that objective by identifying the way you express your dishonesty, your past effort to overcome it, and your present willingness to become radically honest with each other. I recommend that you answer the following questions and discuss your answers with each other.

1. When you are dishonest with your spouse, what kind of liar are you? Are you a protector liar, a trying-to-look-better-than-you-are

liar, an avoid trouble liar, a compulsive liar, or some combination of them?

2. When you are dishonest with your spouse, what do you tend to lie about? Your emotional reactions, your past history, your present activities, your future plans, or some combination of them?

3. What are some of the most important reasons that you are dishonest with your spouse?

4. When you are dishonest with your spouse, what do you typically do?

5. When you are dishonest with your spouse, what hurts your spouse the most?

6. When have you tried to overcome dishonesty with your spouse, and how did you try to do it? What has been the outcome?

7. If you were to decide to be radically honest with your spouse from today forward, would you be able to do it? Why or why not?

8. Are you willing to be radically honest with your spouse? Why or why not?

9. Provide further information that would help you avoid dishonesty in the future.

If you have been dishonest, your spouse may not be entirely aware of it. In the case of an angry outburst, the offended spouse can identify the offense as soon as it happens. But in the case of dishonesty, sometimes the offended spouse does not know that it's occurred until months later when he or she has the evidence of dishonesty firmly in hand. So the first step in overcoming this Love Buster is to reveal it as the monster that it is. If you really want to become honest, you must first reveal the fact that you've been dishonest. And you must reveal the way you tend to be dishonest.

Questions 1 and 2 are particularly helpful in understanding the habits of dishonesty. Knowing the kind of liar you are and what you tend to lie about can help you focus your attention on those habits that need to be changed. That information will assist you in the next step, which is to create a plan to overcome dishonesty and become radically honest.

### Step 2: Create a plan to overcome dishonesty.

To help you formulate this plan, answer the following questions:

1. Describe your dishonesty. Include a description of your feelings, your thoughts and attitudes, and the way you are dishonest. Review the kind of liar you are (a protector liar, a trying-to-look-better-than-you-are liar, an avoid trouble liar, a compulsive liar, or some combination of them) and what you tend to lie about (your emotional reactions, your past history, your present activities, your future plans, or some combination of them).

2. Describe the conditions that seem to trigger your dishonesty. Include physical setting, people present, behavior of those people, and any other relevant conditions.

*If you really want to become honest, you must first reveal the fact that you've been dishonest. And you must reveal the way you tend to be dishonest.*

3. What changes in those conditions described in #2 would help you avoid your dishonesty?

4. Which of the changes in #3 can be made with your spouse's enthusiastic agreement?

5. Describe your plan to change these conditions. Include a deadline to make the change complete. Be certain that your plan has your spouse's enthusiastic support.

6. Which of the changes in #3 cannot be made with your spouse's enthusiastic agreement, or cannot be made at all?

7. Describe your plan to overcome dishonesty when the conditions described in #6 exist. Include a deadline for successful completion of the plan. Be certain that your plan has your spouse's enthusiastic support.

8. How will you measure the success of your plan to overcome dishonesty? Does this measure of success have your spouse's enthusiastic support?

9. If your plan does not succeed within your designated time limit, do you agree to seek professional help in designing and executing an effective plan to protect your spouse from your dishonesty? How will you go about finding that help?

The protector liar is convinced that misinformation is their spouse's best protection—it's the right thing to do. But this person can learn to be honest more quickly when it's realized that honesty, not dishonesty, is really the best protection. So a plan to change a protector liar into a radically honest spouse should begin by letting him or her know that you do not regard any form of dishonesty as protection. Tell your dishonest spouse that you want radical honesty at all costs, even if it upsets you at the time of its revelation. Even then, however, your spouse's habit to lie may be so strong that dishonest slips may be very common at first. That is why it's so important to document your progress, as I will explain later. Slips must be acknowledged as quickly as possible by the dishonest spouse.

Trying-to-look-better-than-you-are liars usually have a great need for admiration, but they feel that what they do is not enough to warrant it. If their spouse is willing to meet that emotional need (see chapter 12 in *His Needs, Her Needs*), that can make it much easier for them to learn to become radically honest. Another way to help this type of liar is to become more integrated into their lives. Steve got away with his lies because his wife, Sally, wasn't aware of what he was doing. The Policy of Radical Honesty gives her the right to check up on him. But that can't be the entire plan. It's ultimately up to the liar to change. And he or she must be able to do something no one else can do: admit any lies as soon as they are made, and correct the statements to make them honest.

The avoid trouble liar is usually faced with two problems: he or she gets into trouble and then lies about it. The "getting in trouble" part is usually the result of failing to follow the Policy of Joint Agreement. Something is done that will upset the spouse if he or she finds out about it. So part of the strategy to overcome avoid trouble lying is to follow the Policy of Joint Agreement in the first place. In chapter 13, I'll introduce a plan to help you achieve that objective. And again, self-monitoring of any instances of dishonesty is an essential part of recovery. Regardless of how disappointed the other spouse may be when a lie has been confessed, it must be done to break the habit of dishonesty.

Compulsive liars are rare in marriage because their deceit, which soon becomes obvious to almost everyone who knows them, usually prevents people from wanting to risk marriage. But if you seem to be a compulsive liar, I suggest obtaining a neurological evaluation since it is often caused by a brain injury or a progressive brain disorder, such as a tumor. Subsequent medical attention may help restore your ability to remember what really happens to you throughout the day. My personal experience trying to help compulsive liars learn how to become honest has been disappointing.

As I've already mentioned, one of the ways to overcome a bad habit is to simply get rid of the conditions that seem to trigger that habit. You may notice, for example, that there are certain people in your life who tend to encourage you to be dishonest with your spouse. Perhaps you find yourself engaging in certain behavior with those people who usually offend your spouse. And then when your spouse asks about what you've been doing, you lie about it. By simply eliminating these people as friends you may find you've eliminated your dishonesty as well.

But you may find that the conditions that seem to trigger your dishonesty can't be changed. For example, financial pressures may tempt you to be dishonest. When you can't pay your bills you are tempted to keep that fact from your spouse. And you simply can't change the condition of your financial pressure.

In that situation you will need to create a strategy where, under those very conditions that tend to make you dishonest, you practice being honest. You explain to your spouse how difficult it is to reveal the fact that you can't pay your bills and involve him or her in all financial decisions. All the money you earn would be deposited into a checking account that your spouse can clearly see. All the bills that you pay are made with your joint enthusiastic agreement. Any unpaid bills are known and agreed to by your spouse.

### Step 3: Document your progress.

When you're ready to put your strategy to overcome dishonesty into action, I encourage you to document your progress. Title a sheet of paper "Dishonesty Worksheet," and use it to list all instances of dishonesty. Generally, the offended spouse completes the worksheet to document progress, but in this case, you and your spouse should complete it together, since there may be instances of your dishonesty that your spouse would not know of if you did not tell him or her.

Indicate the day, date, time, description and type of dishonesty, and circumstances whenever you document an instance of dishonesty. If your strategy to overcome dishonesty is successful, you'll find yourself listing fewer and fewer instances of dishonesty. Eventually you'll get into the habit of being completely honest with your spouse and your spouse will be in the habit of encouraging that honesty by avoiding demands, disrespect, or anger when you are honest.

## Radical Honesty Is Complete Honesty

It goes without saying: false impressions are just as deceitful as outright lies. The purpose of honesty is having the facts in front of you. Without them, you'll fail to solve the simplest marital problems. Why should it make a difference how you fail to reveal the facts to each other, whether by lies or by giving false impressions? Either one will leave your spouse ignorant.

I need to ask probing questions during premarital counseling. Since I know the areas where people tend to give false impressions, that's where I probe most deeply. Since most marital problems originate with serious misconceptions, I do what I can to dig out these little weeds that eventually choke the plant.

You may be giving each other false impressions about your emotional reactions, or your past history, or your present activities, or your plans for the future—or all four! If you are, you may be thinking to yourself that you're not really lying. If your spouse were to ask the right questions, you would tell the truth. But remember why it's important to be honest. Honesty shines a bright light on the road map that leads to solutions to your marital problems. False impressions make the map useless because they obscure the nature of the problem itself. Radical honesty does not simply give honest answers to questions—it provides answers to questions that your spouse may not have even known to ask.

Radical honesty provides a clear road map for marital adjustment. A husband and wife who are radically honest with each other can identify their problems very quickly and, if they know how to negotiate with each other, dispose of them very quickly. Sometimes dishonesty covers up both the problems themselves and the solutions to those problems.

If you are honest, you reveal the facts about how you feel, what you've done, what you're doing, and what you plan to do. The more facts you have, the better you'll understand each other. The more you understand each other, the more likely it is that you'll come up with solutions to your problems. Ed and Jennifer drifted into a loveless marriage because they failed to reveal crucial facts that would have helped them both understand the problems that they faced.

*Radical honesty does not simply give honest answers to questions—it provides answers to questions that your spouse may not have even known to ask.*

Trust is essential in marriage. Without it, intimacy and security are impossible. But trust must be earned. There must be evidence that what you say to each other is true. That evidence is provided every year, every month, every day, and every hour that spouses never lie to each other about anything, always giving each other everything that they know about themselves.

## Key Principles

**The Policy of Radical Honesty:** Reveal to your spouse as much information about yourself as you know—your thoughts, feelings, habits, likes, dislikes, personal history, daily activities, and plans for the future.

Radical honesty is essential in marriage because (1) it provides a clear road map for marital adjustment, (2) honesty is an important emotional need, and (3) dishonesty in any form is a Love Buster—it causes massive Love Bank withdrawals.

Learn to be in the habit of radical honesty by (1) understanding how and why the habit of dishonesty has established itself, (2) creating a plan that addresses the type of dishonesty you have, and

(3) holding yourself accountable by creating a worksheet that lists instances of dishonesty.

## Consider This . . . ——————————————

1. What is the Policy of Radical Honesty and what are the four parts of the policy? Do you agree that you should both follow this policy? If so, why? If not, why not? You will probably find that you are likely to want your spouse to be honest with you more than you want to be honest with your spouse.

2. I have created a Personal History Questionnaire that you can download free of charge from the Questionnaires section of the marriagebuilders.com website. Make two copies, one for each of you. After answering the questions, give them to each other to read. Then take some time going over them together, answering any questions that either of you may have regarding new information that you may not have previously known.

# 12

## Independent Behavior: *Part 1*

### Who Wants to Live with an Inconsiderate Jerk?

Brian came to my office with his wife, Kay, wanting to know why she wouldn't make love to him. In my interview with Kay, she explained that the spark was gone—she simply didn't feel like being intimate with Brian the way she had in the past. What had seemed almost effortless to her in the beginning of their marriage now seemed almost impossible.

As I pursued the problem further, I didn't find any of the most common causes for her lack of sexual interest. Brian had never demanded sex, or criticized her for her lack of interest. And there was nothing wrong with the way he made love with her—he certainly knew how to be a good lover. Kay's problem was that she no longer felt emotionally connected to him. For her, that was reason enough to avoid lovemaking entirely.

While dating, Brian and Kay were a team. They planned their week together, they enjoyed the same recreational activities together, they volunteered for weekend community projects together, and they talked or texted each other throughout every day. They were each other's best friends and were together as much as possible.

But after marriage, they began to drift apart. They didn't plan their week together anymore, or spend their recreational time together, or volunteer for community projects together. Texting and phone conversations throughout the day almost came to a complete halt. What had been a partnership became a sole proprietorship.

Kay realized that something was wrong, and tried to do something about it. In her effort to become a part of Brian's life again, she argued with him, telling him that he was being selfish by not considering her feelings in the decisions he made. Occasionally she lost her temper when he would keep what he was doing from her. But he told her that they had become too enmeshed while dating, and that he needed a little breathing room. While his perspective offended Kay, she eventually accepted it, and tried to follow a more independent lifestyle herself. When that happened, their arguing ended.

The result of their efforts to be independent ruined the primary reason that Kay had wanted to make love with Brian—her feeling of oneness with him. For Kay, their lovemaking was a reflection of their partnership in life. But when Brian decided that partnership was too restrictive and confining for him, she lost her emotional connection.

But Brian's decision to live his life more independently did more than break Kay's emotional connection to him. It also made massive Love Bank withdrawals every time he made an independent decision. His choice of friends, his recreational activities, his financial decisions, his daily schedule, and a host of other decisions he made that did not consider Kay's feelings or interests all whittled away at his Love Bank account until there were no love units left. Then, his account plunged deeply into the red. Kay was not just disconnected: she didn't even like Brian anymore.

## What's Wrong with Independence?

At first glance, independent behavior in marriage might seem not just desirable, but essential for a healthy and happy marriage. After all, who wants to be clingy and dependent? And who wants a spouse who is clingy and dependent—unable to do anything by themselves or make any decisions of their own?

But independent behavior is not the only alternative to unhealthy dependency. Another far superior alternative is what I call **interdependency**, which is behaving in ways that take each other's feelings into account.

It all goes back to what I have been repeating throughout this book—almost everything you do in marriage will affect your spouse either positively or negatively, whether or not you intended to do so. If you want a marriage that makes both of you happy, you must pay close attention to the ways your behavior affects each other. And then you must learn to behave in ways that make each other happy, and avoid making each other unhappy.

*Interdependent behavior recognizes that, in marriage, activities must be mutually acceptable to guarantee the protection of each spouse's interests and feelings.*

For purposes of this discussion, let me give you my definition of independent behavior in marriage—it's the activities of a spouse that are conceived and executed as if the other spouse did not even exist. It's independent in that it ignores the interests and feelings of the other spouse.

**Inter**dependent behavior, on the other hand, is the activities of a spouse that are conceived and executed with the interests of both spouses in mind. It recognizes that, in marriage, activities must be mutually acceptable to guarantee the protection of each spouse's interests and feelings.

| Independent Behavior | Interdependent Behavior |
|---|---|
| Conceived and executed as if the other spouse did not exist | Conceived and executed with the interests of both spouses in mind |
| Ignores interests and feelings of the other spouse | Mutually acceptable activities guarantee the protection of each spouse's interests and feelings |

It's the difference between a sole proprietorship and a partnership. If you own 100 percent of a business, you have the right to make your own business decisions. But if you have a partner who owns an equal share of the business, you should come to an agreement before making decisions. Otherwise the business relationship will suffer, and the business itself will suffer. Marriage should be a partnership because decisions that are not mutually agreeable hurt the relationship and the productivity of the marriage.

## The Rooms of a House

I used an imaginary house to help Brian understand how his lifestyle affected Kay. Each room in this house represented one of the roles he played in life. There was a career room, a leisure activity room, a family room, a religious practices room, and, yes, a marriage room.

Brian's career room was filled with furniture and projects designed to make him a successful production manager. His leisure activity room contained golf equipment and immediate access to friends who enjoy playing golf with him. The family room contained video games and a television set that he used when he spent time with his children. His religious practices room had been made into an Episcopal chapel. And right in the middle of his marriage room was a big bed.

As he made his way through an average day, Brian would visit the rooms representing the roles he played. When in any one room, he would keep the doors to the other rooms closed so that he could focus his undivided attention on the role he played in that room. He found that he did his best when he avoided the distractions of other roles he played in life.

Since Brian regarded Kay and her interests as a distraction, he relegated her to only one room in his house—the marriage room—and that made her feel neglected and resentful. While it was true that Brian gave Kay his undivided attention when he met her in the marriage room and made a special effort to meet her needs, she felt totally ignored the rest of the time. She wanted him to invite her into every room, so that she would be fully integrated into his life, but he refused. Instead, he wanted her to create a house of her own with a marriage room where he could join her.

So that's what Kay tried to do. In her house, she also had a career room, but it was outfitted with furniture and projects designed to make her a successful accountant. Her leisure activity room was full of gardening books and supplies. Her family activity room contained bicycles and sporting equipment used when she took her children to their after-school sporting events. Her religious practices room was a Baptist chapel. And in her marriage room, there was . . . nothing. She had emotionally bailed out of the marriage and excluded Brian from all of her rooms. And to make her point perfectly clear, she refused to sleep with him. In their real house, she slept in a separate room.

Of course, the problems between Brian and Kay were about much more than sex. Kay's refusal to make love may have been the first symptom of a bad marriage that got Brian's attention. But there had been plenty of other warning signs before that. She had begged him to spend weekends with her, instead of golfing with his friends. She cried when he refused to participate in their children's school projects and activities. And she felt like a widow taking her children to church each week without their father. His entire lifestyle made her unhappy and caused huge Love Bank withdrawals. And if his independent behavior had continued much longer, she would have divorced him.

### Why Is Independent Behavior So Tempting?

Those who engage in independent behavior often think that it actually strengthens a marriage. Without it, they would feel trapped and suffocated. Who they choose as friends, what they do on the job, where they spend their spare time, and even how they pay their bills—these are choices that they believe no one, not even their spouse, should interfere with. They view any attempt to take away their "freedom of choice" as controlling and manipulative, a marriage-wrecker for sure.

Independent behavior also feeds on the mistaken belief of some that it actually makes spouses more attractive to each other. If clingy dependency is viewed as the only alternative to independent behavior, they have a point. But they ignore the fact that neither of those options creates a happy marriage. It's only interdependent behavior that can help them achieve long-term marital satisfaction.

Another reason that independent behavior is tempting is that some spouses believe they should be blindly trusted in the decisions they make. If their spouse challenges their decisions, they consider it to be disrespectful. In fact, many of my clients have tried to misapply the Love Buster category of disrespectful judgments to their spouse's complaints regarding their independent behavior. "If you respected me, you wouldn't challenge my decisions," is a common defense that tries to mask what is actually thoughtlessness.

But the most important reason independent behavior is tempting in marriage is that it's instinctive. You are born with a predisposition to make decisions that are good for you regardless of how it affects your spouse. Unless you resist that predisposition, whenever you ignore your spouse's interests and feelings, you'll be eroding the love he or she has for you, and you'll be destroying your emotional bond.

Brian felt that what he did in the rooms of his imaginary house should not have any impact on Kay, because the doors were closed and she was not invited to participate. But present or not, everything he did, even in the privacy of his rooms, affected her one way or another. When he went golfing with his friends, he withdrew love units from her Love Bank. His work schedule also upset her, as did the way he chose to interact with their children. Even his differences in religious practices bothered her. Keeping her in the hallways of his house did not prevent her from feeling the impact of each independent behavior.

Slowly but surely Kay was finding Brian's lifestyle increasingly intolerable. Eventually she woke up to the realization that they had nothing but their children to keep them together. And she was beginning to think that even that was not enough.

Unfortunately, Brian and Kay are not very different from many married couples today when it comes to independent behavior. And this Love Buster threatens to tear many of them apart. But of all the Love Busters we've discussed so far, this one usually sneaks in under the radar. For many couples, they don't see how destructive their independent behavior is to the health of their marriage until it's too late.

### Independent Behavior Starts Fights . . . and Ends Fights

In most marriages, independent behavior causes fights. When you behave as if your spouse doesn't exist, your spouse won't tolerate it at first, and will go to war with you. That's how Kay reacted to Brian's independent behavior. But after countless arguments that never resolved anything, Kay stopped fighting. In fact, she made very few demands of Brian, was rarely disrespectful, and never had an angry outburst. Instead of fighting, Kay simply let Brian's independent behavior drain her Love

Bank, and when it was deeply in the red, she started to consider divorce as a real possibility for her.

To some extent, Kay felt that Brian had the right to make independent decisions. So she could see no solution to their problem. While in theory she wanted to become emotionally reconnected to Brian, she couldn't see herself joining him in each room of his house. By this time, she was even unwilling to invite him into her rooms—she wasn't attracted to him anymore. And yet, if she was to become emotionally bonded to him again, they had to become integrated into every aspect of each other's lives again.

I told Brian that if he wanted a happy marriage, Kay's feelings and interests had to be considered in every decision he made. As equal partners, they should create a completely integrated lifestyle, enjoyable for both of them. That, in turn, would lead to the emotional bonding Kay needed to restore the sexual relationship they had once enjoyed. And, more importantly, it would turn a divorce in the making into the partnership that they should have had all along.

## Key Principles

**Independent behavior** is the activities of one spouse that are conceived and executed as if the other spouse did not exist.

**Interdependent behavior** is the activities of a spouse that are conceived and executed with both spouses' interests in mind.

Whenever you ignore your spouse's interests and feelings, you are eroding the love he or she has for you, and you are destroying your emotional bond.

## Consider This . . .

1. Is independent behavior a problem in your marriage? To answer that question, complete the independent behavior page (page 216) of the Love Busters Questionnaire in Appendix B. Make

two enlarged copies, one for each of you, so that you will have enough space to write your answers.

2. Think of a few instances of independent behavior that have been a problem for you in the past, but that are no longer a problem for either of you. How did you go about ridding yourself of those Love Busters? Think of other examples that are still a problem for one of you. What are you presently doing to try to overcome them?

3. Have you tried to justify independent behavior? Do you feel that you should have the right to make independent decisions, that those decisions will make you more attractive to your spouse, and that when your spouse challenges your decisions he or she is being disrespectful? Are there other arguments you have used? Regardless of your arguments that support independent behavior, what's the bottom line?

4. Describe each of your own imaginary houses. Which rooms are easy for you to both enter and which are more difficult to enter? Which are locked shut to the other spouse? What are the advantages and disadvantages of inviting each other into all of your rooms?

# 13

## Independent Behavior: *Part 2*

### How to Turn Independent Behavior into Interdependent Behavior

Two steps were required to help Brian and Kay create an integrated lifestyle. First, they had to invite each other into all of the rooms of their imaginary houses, and then they had to come to an agreement as to how each room should be decorated.

The first step required them to apply the Policy of Radical Honesty to their marriage: *Reveal to your spouse as much information about yourself as you know—your thoughts, feelings, habits, likes, dislikes, personal history, daily activities, and plans for the future.* I introduced this rule to you in chapter 11 to help you avoid the Love Buster of dishonesty. But this rule does more than that. It also gives couples a clear and accurate description of what they are doing throughout the day. It describes what goes on in each room of their house. It's an invitation to enter all of the rooms.

At first, Kay was more reluctant than Brian to reveal all of her daily activities. So he took the initiative by revealing his complete schedule to her, along with a description of what he would be doing and who would be joining him. He let her know where he would be, and a telephone number where he could be reached in an emergency. His willingness to invite her into his rooms eventually encouraged her to invite him into her rooms as well. By providing information to each other about their daily activities and plans for the future, they were swept into the inner recesses of the lives that had previously been hidden from each other.

But they needed to complete a second step before their lives could be integrated and they could become equal partners again. They had to agree on what would happen in those rooms. This step required them to follow another rule that I introduced to you earlier—the Policy of Joint Agreement: *Never do anything without an enthusiastic agreement between you and your spouse.*

*But now we have a different use for the Policy of Joint Agreement. Instead of using it to prevent a selfish demand, trying to make your spouse do something for you, we will be using it to prevent independent behavior, trying to do something that your spouse would object to your doing.*

In chapter 5, the Policy of Joint Agreement was used to help a couple change selfish demands into thoughtful requests. Whenever one spouse wanted something from the other, this policy prohibited them from trying to force the other to do whatever they wanted. Instead, they were to find a way to obtain what they needed from each other in a considerate and thoughtful way. They were to meet each other's needs with enthusiastic agreement.

But now we have a different use for the Policy of Joint Agreement. Instead of using it to prevent a selfish demand, trying to make your spouse do something for you, we will be using it to prevent independent behavior, trying to do something that your spouse would object to your doing.

The policy works well in both situations. When you want something from each other, it helps you think of ways to obtain it that will strengthen your marriage, instead of weakening it. And the same is true when you want to do something that your spouse would not approve of your doing: it helps you think of other ways of doing it, or other alternative activities, that would make you both happy. Instead of weakening your marriage with thoughtless activities, it helps you strengthen your marriage with thoughtful activities.

## The Policy of Joint Agreement and Interdependent Behavior

The word "anything" in the Policy of Joint Agreement means that all rooms of a house and everything in each room are subject to scrutiny and possible replacement. In other words, if Brian were to follow the policy, he had to think about Kay's reaction to *everything* he did, not just what went on in the "marriage room," or even just a few of the other rooms. She had to be consulted about what went on in every part of his life. And Kay had to do the same after inviting Brian into her rooms. Did they approve of each other's activities? If either of them were not enthusiastic, changes would be in order. All of the rooms had to eventually contain lifestyle activities that they would both enthusiastically accept.

It's common for spouses to view the prospect of redecoration with horror. "I have my rooms furnished just the way I like them," would be a common reaction. "When my spouse starts throwing things out and bringing things in, it will not be the comfortable room I carefully created."

The Policy of Joint Agreement addresses that issue by requiring all changes to be **mutually** agreeable. In other words, Kay could not create a new lifestyle unless Brian was as sold on it as she was, and vice versa. Neither had the right to force each other into a room that was uncomfortable. Instead, they had to create a lifestyle that was comfortable for both of them.

Brian wanted to know why I insisted on an "enthusiastic" agreement. He felt that a simple agreement would be a big step in the right direction—why insist on enthusiasm?

I explained that marital agreements are often coerced or self-sacrificing. I didn't want either of them to think that they had to agree just to get along, and I didn't want them to sacrifice their interests so that the other could have what he or she wanted. Kay was not simply a guest in Brian's rooms and Brian was not a guest in Kay's rooms. They were equal partners with the right to rearrange the rooms to make them mutually comfortable.

The Policy of Joint Agreement prevents fights in marriage. It makes absolutely no sense to try to force a spouse to do something when enthusiastic agreement is the objective. No one is expected to suffer. Both are expected to thrive because only win-win outcomes should be tolerated. It isn't just Kay's enthusiastic agreement that is required before a decision is made. Brian's enthusiastic agreement is required as well. There are to be no activities or furniture in any of his rooms that she does not also enthusiastically support. The goal of marriage is to become united in purpose and spirit, not to overpower or control each other.

## The Policy of Joint Agreement and Resentment

The default condition of the Policy of Joint Agreement is to do nothing until an enthusiastic agreement is reached. That can certainly lead to resentment while trying to find that agreement. And Brian was acutely aware of it. It meant that he couldn't do what he wanted to do until he had Kay's approval. He felt trapped by the Policy.

So I had to explain to Brian why the resentment he felt at following the Policy of Joint Agreement was not as bad as the resentment that Kay felt when he violated the Policy by doing whatever he pleased. His resentment would last only as long as it took to resolve the conflict. Once an enthusiastic agreement was reached, all thoughts of what he could have been doing would vanish. Kay's resentment, on the other hand, would last forever. Years after his violation, she would remember that what he wanted to do was so important to him, that he disregarded her feelings and interests. His lack of care would stir up resentment whenever she thought about it.

But to help make my point more acceptable to Brian, I added that the default condition, to do nothing, was not the resolution to a conflict. Instead, it was what you are to do while trying to resolve the conflict.

I had to agree with Brian that the resentment of doing nothing could actually be as great as the resentment caused by doing whatever you please if the conflict is never resolved. So he and Kay had to not only agree to follow the Policy of Joint Agreement, but also to agree to put the conflict on the front burner until it was resolved.

Kay was very willing to find resolutions to conflicts as quickly as possible. So she and Brian were both ready to learn how to reach enthusiastic agreements by following the Four Guidelines for Successful Negotiation in Marriage.

## Using the Four Guidelines for Successful Negotiation in Marriage to Become Interdependent

When you decide to become interdependent, you will not have fewer conflicts—you will have more of them. At least there will seem to be more conflicts because you will address each of them as they arise. In fact, you will welcome them if you can dispatch them as fast as they come up.

Joyce and I have at least one conflict every hour we're together. And yet we have a terrific marriage. That's because it's not conflicts that make a marriage miserable. Marriages fail because couples don't know how to resolve conflicts quickly when they arise. Since Joyce and I know how to handle conflicts the right way, they actually make our marriage stronger, not weaker. Whenever we have a conflict, an area of weakness is identified, and when we resolve the conflict, our marriage is strengthened.

When I introduced the Policy of Joint Agreement in chapter 5 to help you protect your spouse from your selfish demands, I also showed you how to come to an enthusiastic agreement by using the Four Guidelines for Successful Negotiation in Marriage. Those Four Guidelines can also be used when it comes to protecting your spouse from your independent behavior. In the case of thoughtful requests, they are used to help you motivate your spouse to **do** something for you with enthusiastic agreement. But in the case of interdependent behavior they are used to help you **avoid doing** something that your spouse would find offensive, and replace it with an acceptable alternative.

So I will reintroduce to you the Four Guidelines for Successful Negotiation in Marriage as the ways you should create interdependent behavior.

## Guideline 1: Set ground rules to make your discussion pleasant and safe.

Arguing never resolved conflicts for Kay during the early years of their marriage. So she was on board when I told her that all of their discussions had to be **pleasant** and **safe**. It had to be pleasant in that she should try to make sure that she and Brian were enjoying the conversation. And it had to be safe by completely avoiding selfish demands, disrespectful judgments, or angry outbursts. They were both to maintain zero tolerance for these three destructive habits, but it would be more difficult for her because she had so much resentment over his past thoughtlessness toward her. I advised them to postpone their discussion if either of them failed to keep it pleasant or safe, and resume it after they had a chance to regain emotional control.

## Guideline 2: Introduce the conflict and try to understand each other's perspective.

Kay and Brian had so many conflicts to resolve that it was difficult to pick just one to serve as an example of how the others would be handled. Brian wanted us to begin with the problem that brought him to my office: Kay's reluctance to make love with him. But I suggested that they begin with a conflict that would be easier to resolve and might also make her sexual reluctance easier to address. Eventually they agreed to try to resolve the conflict they had over recreational activities. I thought that if they could solve that problem, they might also solve their sexual problem at the same time, or at least make some progress toward solving it.

Brian was an avid golfer and Kay did not enjoy the sport. Besides, throughout their marriage, he had made it clear that nothing would interfere with his tee time, which meant to Kay that golf was more important to him than she was. Every time she heard the word "golf," it made her angry.

The Policy of Joint Agreement, which they had both decided to follow on at least a trial basis, made it clear that Brian could not engage in any recreational activity, golf included, unless he had Kay's enthusiastic agreement. And with her resentment about his past enjoyment of the sport at her expense, she could not imagine ever being enthusiastic about it.

In the past, they would have defined the conflict as, *Brian wants to play golf this Saturday, but Kay wants him to go for a bike ride with the family.* But I wanted them to state the conflict in broader terms without actually suggesting a resolution in the definition itself. So they came up with, *what are the recreational activities in which each of us can participate?* In other words, what can we do recreationally that will make us both happy?

During this phase of problem-solving, radical honesty is essential in understanding each other's perspective. But you should be careful to avoid being critical of each other's opinions, and be able to understand them well enough to be able to repeat them accurately to each other.

Kay was quick to explain how resentful she felt about Brian's golfing, and Brian was just as quick to explain how much he enjoyed it, and really didn't have anything else in life to look forward to each week. Instead of attacking each other's perspectives, they tried to empathize with each other. She tried to understand that if he really didn't enjoy being with her and the children on weekends, it was reasonable to use golf as an escape. He tried to understand how she would feel abandoned by him, leaving her alone with the children while he was off having an enjoyable and restful weekend.

One of the biggest mistakes couples make in this phase of problem-solving is to be disrespectful. Many people think that their honesty must include their criticism of an opposing opinion. But radical honesty does not include disrespectful judgments, even when you feel like being disrespectful. You're not being dishonest when you keep your critical thoughts to yourself—you're being respectful.

Disrespect is a poison pill when it comes to negotiating. If Kay had told Brian that he was being selfish to play golf when the family needed him to be with them, it would have ended the discussion and eliminated all efforts to come to an enthusiastic agreement. The same would have been true if Brian had criticized Kay for failing to see how important it was for him to have some escape over the weekend. On the other hand, their effort to try to understand each other and to try to accommodate each other's perspective encouraged further discussion.

### Guideline 3: Brainstorm with abandon.

For many conflicts, like the one that Kay and Brian faced, it isn't easy to find a resolution that accommodates the perspectives of both spouses. So they needed to give their brains a chance to do some of the hard work by letting the problem incubate.

Kay wanted to engage in recreational activities that would unite her with Brian. Brian wanted to engage in recreational activities that would enable him to escape his responsibilities. What recreational activity would enable them to do both?

When a conflict is first defined, a mutually agreeable resolution may not occur to either of you immediately. You may need time to brainstorm about possible solutions. Use your smartphone or carry a notepad around with you so that you can record solutions as they occur to you. It may take days before you have accumulated several possibilities. But remember, whatever you record should take both you and your spouse's perspectives into account simultaneously.

Before marriage, Kay and Brian had engaged in many recreational activities together that they had both enjoyed. When he had been with her, he didn't feel pressure or responsibility. He felt as if he was escaping all of that—with her! But after they married, and especially after the children arrived, he didn't feel the same way. He felt responsible for her and the children whenever they were together.

Kay's primary goal was to feel united with Brian, the way she felt before they were married. They had done everything together with such ease and she wanted that back again. For her, involving the children in what they did was not as important as doing things together.

Every day they wrote down ideas that might work for them, and every evening they discussed those ideas with each other. They explained why an idea would work, and why it would not work, with respect and honesty.

Within a few days they both began to consider spending all day Saturday doing something recreationally with each other without their children. They considered it to be a temporary solution to their problem that would someday include the whole family. But for now, they felt it would be the best way to restore their emotional connection to each other.

They each made a list of recreational activities that they would enjoy, and then swapped lists and rated each other's activities according to how much they would enjoy doing them. They came up with a list of six activities that they would both enjoy doing together: visiting neighboring towns, bike riding, hiking in nearby parks, playing tennis, exercising and swimming at a local YMCA, and watching sporting events. Both sets of parents agreed to care for their children on alternate weekends so that they could put their plan into action.

### Guideline 4: Find the solution that provides a mutually enthusiastic agreement.

Neither Kay nor Brian were sure that spending time together on Saturdays engaged in one or more of the six activities would work. Kay was not sure that she would enjoy being with a husband who was wishing he were playing golf, and Brian was not sure that the time would actually make him feel relaxed and free of pressure. But they decided to try it for a month with the agreement that if it didn't work, they would go back to the drawing board.

The plan worked. Kay was very encouraged by Brian's willingness to join her in his escape from responsibilities, and Brian was surprised to discover that being with Kay made the activities they had chosen very enjoyable for him—so much so that he really didn't miss playing golf that much. What they enjoyed the most was the time they spent at the YMCA together. They both wanted to keep physically fit, and by doing it together they were able to achieve personal and marital objectives all at once.

But if Brian had felt that he still missed playing golf too much to continue the test, or if Kay felt that it was not helping her feel bonded to him, they would have gone back to brainstorming. Their goal was to solve their recreational problem in a way that made them both happy with the solution, and until that was achieved, they would continue to test various alternatives.

## How Easy Is It?

Couples who already have an interdependent lifestyle have little or no trouble following the Policy of Radical Honesty and the Policy of Joint Agreement because they have learned how to behave in sensitive and caring ways regardless of the roles they play.

But couples like Brian and Kay with independent lifestyles have more difficulty following these policies at first. They are accustomed to doing what they please, regardless of its effect on each other, and then lying about it if it's objectionable, especially when they're playing certain roles. But if they can follow these policies for just a few weeks, like Brian and Kay did, they begin to see how their dishonesty and thoughtlessness have created the emotional distance they are experiencing. As they try to apply these policies to each of their daily plans and activities, they begin to feel cared for by each other and are encouraged by each other's thoughtfulness. Over time, their emotional bonding becomes increasingly secure, and the policies become easier and easier to follow as they learn how to make thoughtful choices.

*Those who follow the Policy of Joint Agreement think about their spouse throughout the day, because as they make decisions they ask themselves how their spouse would feel.*

Those who follow the Policy of Joint Agreement think about their spouse throughout the day, because as they make decisions they ask themselves how their spouse would feel. Phone calls are made whenever there is any doubt. And by giving radically honest answers to each other's questions, they become increasingly sensitive to each other's feelings.

If spouses consider each other's feelings in every decision they make, asking each other when there is any uncertainty, they eventually create a compatible lifestyle. The Policy of Joint Agreement and the Policy of Radical Honesty help create understanding, emotional bonding, intimacy, and romantic love in marriage. Over time, they experience what every couple hopes to create in marriage: a loving and compatible relationship.

By the time Brian and Kay had invited each other into every room in their houses and had made adjustments that created a mutually comfortable lifestyle, Kay could no longer even imagine leaving Brian. That's because she wasn't standing in the hallways of his house feeling like a stranger. All his rooms were her rooms as well, and she was welcomed into his entire home as his cherished life partner.

As I had expected, once Kay was fully integrated into Brian's life, the issue of sex simply disappeared. As soon as she felt emotionally bonded to Brian again, she was very willing to resume what had been a great sexual experience for her before he had decided to make independent decisions.

### The Choice Is Yours

Marriages usually go one of two ways: nature takes its course and marital compatibility is eventually lost, or a couple can decide to build compatibility by eliminating independent behavior and replacing it with interdependent behavior. My years of marriage counseling have taught me a very important lesson: unless couples create compatibility throughout their marriage, the compatibility they had at the time of their wedding will be destroyed.

When couples divorce or separate because they're "incompatible," does this mean they were doomed from the start? Is there some basic personality clash they just can't overcome? No, it just means they've failed to *create* compatibility. Very likely they developed interests and activities independently of each other. They weren't thoughtful enough to try to include each other in the most relevant and enjoyable moments of their lives.

What a shame! It doesn't have to be that way. A marriage, a family, and personal happiness can be saved if a couple would apply thought and consideration to the decisions they make.

I have created a twelve-week home-study course for couples to learn how to resolve conflicts the right way—with a win-win outcome. This course focuses a couple's attention on the conflicts that other couples face, and gives them the skills to resolve those conflicts. Then, after successfully learning those skills, the couple is ready to tackle their own conflicts with an awareness of how their emotional reactions can get in the way of wise decision-making.

If you have trouble finding win-win outcomes to the conflicts you face, I encourage you to read my book, *He Wins, She Wins: Learning the Art of Marital Negotiation*, and follow my twelve-week home study course, found in its companion, *He Wins, She Wins Workbook*.

When you learn how to resolve conflicts using the Four Guidelines for Successful Negotiation in Marriage, you will not only be able to get what you need from each other, but you will also create a lifestyle that makes you compatible. And you won't be arguing with each other—you'll be discussing your conflicts safely and enjoyably.

## Key Principles

Two policies help create interdependence: (1) the **Policy of Radical Honesty** (reveal to your spouse as much information about yourself as you know—your thoughts, feelings, habits, likes, dislikes, personal history, daily activities, and plans for the future), and (2) the **Policy of Joint Agreement** (never do anything without an enthusiastic agreement between you and your spouse).

Unless couples create compatibility throughout their marriage through interdependent behavior, the compatibility they had at the time of their wedding will be destroyed.

There are two types of resentment that the Policy of Joint Agreement can create: resentment of the one following the policy by doing nothing, and resentment of the other spouse when the policy is not followed. The first can disappear as soon as an enthusiastic agreement is reached, while the second can last forever.

The **Four Guidelines for Successful Negotiation in Marriage** help couples resolve conflicts the right way—with honesty and thoughtfulness.

## Consider This . . .

1. An invitation to enter each room in your imaginary house is not enough to build compatibility in marriage. What must you do after you invite each other in?

2. How do the Four Guidelines to Successful Negotiation in Marriage help eliminate existing independent behavior and create interdependent behavior? How do they, along with the Policy of Joint Agreement, help prevent the creation of new independent behavior?

# 14

## Annoying Habits: *Part 1*

### Who Wants to Live with a Dripping Faucet?

Long before she married Mike, Sharon knew that some of his habits irritated her. For instance, she didn't like the way he sat in a chair. She admired men who sat straight and tall, giving the impression that they were alert and attentive. When a man slouched in his chair, it reminded her of some of her lazy relatives.

But slouching was Mike's specialty—especially when he came home after work and parked in front of the TV.

"Mike, it really bothers me when you sit like that," she told him when they were newlyweds. "Please sit up in the chair."

Mike straightened up and continued watching television with a better posture, but a few minutes later he slumped back into the same position.

When Sharon returned to the room, she was always very disappointed. "Why do you sit like that, when you know it bothers me?"

Mike would quickly straighten up and say, "Oh, I'm sorry."

"You can't possibly be sorry. You just don't care how I feel."

"Look, Sharon," he'd answer, getting a little irritated. "I've had a hard day at work. Just don't look at me, and you'll feel much better."

Sharon would sometimes leave the room in tears, but Mike would be too absorbed in TV to notice. At first, her tears reflected her anger toward Mike, but after a while she began to doubt herself.

*It's such a small thing*, she thought. *He needs to relax after work, and I'm just being selfish to expect him to sit in his chair a certain way.*

So she decided to keep her feelings to herself. Whenever she saw Mike slumped in his chair, it still annoyed her but she didn't say anything. While the marriage seemed peaceful, Mike was losing love units with each slouch.

He didn't know what was happening to his Love Bank account, and Sharon may not have been fully aware of it either. She didn't want to nag him about it because she felt he had a right to sit any way he chose, but still it bothered her. As time went on, Mike developed other annoying habits, such as chewing ice and spitting it back into his glass, but as with his sitting posture, Sharon felt she had no right to change him.

When they came to see me for counseling, Sharon was in withdrawal and wanted a separation. She wouldn't tell Mike what was bothering her—she simply told him that they weren't right for each other.

Mike's poor posture had become only one example of many habits that made him an almost constant irritant to Sharon. She could hardly tolerate being with him for more than a few minutes at a time, because that's how long it took before another one of his annoying habits appeared. Though she didn't believe in divorce, she just had to get away from Mike and his bad habits.

Yet Mike's "bad" habits were all essentially innocent. They all fell into the same category as his sitting posture. His eating habits, his tone of voice when he disciplined the children, phrases he overused, and the mess he left around the house were simply mannerisms—the ways that he did things. None of these habits were "evil" or intentionally offensive, and Sharon knew this. Another woman might not react the same way, and would be delighted to have him for a husband. But his behavior drove Sharon up a wall. Though she felt guilty about her reaction, it had become so strong and negative that she was sure she'd go crazy unless they separated.

**Why Are We So Annoying?**

When was the last time your spouse did something that annoyed you? Last week? Yesterday? An hour ago? If you're male, the answer is probably "last week," if at all. But if you're female, it's more likely to be "this very minute."

I've found that women usually find men more annoying than men find women. It is probably due to the differences in their brains. A man's brain has fewer connections between the left and right hemispheres. The corpus callosum, the band of fibers connecting them, is larger for women. And there's evidence for more connections between neurons in a woman's brain.

These and other differences may account for women tending to be more aware of what goes on around them, especially what their husbands are doing. But, male or female, our annoying habits draw love units out of our spouse's Love Bank every time.

As a marriage counselor, I tell couples that eliminating annoying habits will improve their marriages. This is not rocket science. It only makes sense that you'll get along better if you stop doing things that drive each other to distraction. But you'd be amazed how many couples just don't get it.

"If Sharon just accepted me for who I am," Mike suggested, "she wouldn't mind it when I pick my teeth after a meal."

"Picking his teeth with his finger," Sharon added. "And by the time he really gets into it, he's got his whole fist in his mouth."

Spouses like Mike often sit in my office and try to convince me that they should be able to do whatever they please—that the objecting spouse should adjust to the annoying habits. But if they were the ones annoyed, it would be a different story.

When *we're* annoyed, we usually think others are being inconsiderate, particularly when we've explained how it bothers us and they continue to do it. But when our behavior annoys *others*, we often feel that we have a right to persist, expecting others to adjust to us.

I often wish I could swap spouses' minds: Mike becomes Sharon for a day and feels what Sharon feels when he picks his teeth. If he could

167

only know *how* annoying his habits are to her, surely he would try to become more considerate. He might argue that it wouldn't bother him if Sharon picked her teeth, but that's not the point. If he could feel what Sharon feels, he would understand why she wants him to change.

So one reason we are annoying is that we don't feel what our spouse feels. As a counselor, I try to help couples become more empathetic—see situations through each other's eyes. Sometimes that helps motivate spouses to overcome annoying habits.

But there is another reason that some of us persist in our annoying habits—we often want our spouse to love us for who we are, not what we do. *I'm not trying to make my spouse feel bad. I'm just being myself,* we might argue. *It's up to my spouse to accept me for who I am. If he or she expects me to change, it must mean that my spouse doesn't really care about the real me.*

Who is the "real" you? It certainly isn't the accumulation of habits you happen to have at any given moment, because those habits are continually changing. Sometimes our habits are changed by design, and sometimes circumstances simply change our habits for us. But we don't change our identity whenever we change a habit. I'm the same person regardless of how I sit in a chair or how I eat. So if I can convince you that your habits are not sacred, that they don't represent characteristics of your identity that will be forever lost if you change them, I can then help you avoid needless loss of love units by simply changing some of your habits: those that your spouse finds annoying.

### Habits That Bother Your Spouse Unintentionally Have to Go

If you want to stay in love, you *must* pay close attention to the way that you affect each other. Your marriage just won't work if you ignore that reality. Whether they're intentional or not, habits affect the love you have for each other. So if your spouse finds some of your habits annoying, they simply have to go. Otherwise your marriage won't be what you want it to be.

Because annoying habits usually have this element of innocence, couples generally don't view them with the same seriousness as, say, angry outbursts, which are an intentional effort to hurt the other spouse. And I would agree with that analysis. Angry outbursts are a show-stopper. You simply cannot solve your problems as long as they exist.

*Whether they're intentional or not, habits affect the love you have for each other.*

But if you're to consider the total number of love units lost, it can be argued that annoying habits might actually withdraw more love units than angry outbursts. While angry outbursts might occur only once every six months, annoying habits are unrelenting, day after day, week after week, month after month. Your annoying habits and the annoying habits of your spouse slowly but surely drain your Love Bank. If you and your spouse don't consider them seriously, your Love Bank is going to be like a sieve. Regardless of how fast you keep pouring love units into that Love Bank, they may drain out even faster unless annoying habits are eliminated.

### What's the Difference Between Annoying Habits and Independent Behavior?

Technically, all Love Busters are annoying. But we generally wouldn't consider, say, an angry outburst as just an annoying habit. It may be annoying, but there is so much more to it that it stands alone in its own category. The same can be said for selfish demands, disrespectful judgments, and dishonesty.

But it's not as easy to separate annoying behavior from independent behavior. Is playing golf an annoying habit or independent behavior? What is it about independent behavior that lets it stand alone as its own category?

The answer to that question is in the definition of independent behavior. It's planned and executed without consideration of the other spouse's interests or feelings. While independent behavior is certainly annoying, what makes it stand out is that it's planned.

Playing golf is a scheduled event, so it qualifies as independent behavior if it's done without a spouse's enthusiastic agreement. Mike's slouching, on the other hand, is not scheduled. He simply does it because he's in the habit of doing it. No one needs to remind him that it's time to slouch. It's never something that he would plan to do.

Granted, some independent behavior may not actually appear on a schedule. But there is always some planning involved, at least at some point in time.

The reason that I'm making this point is that the ways to overcome independent behavior and annoying habits are very different. In the case of independent behavior, the event is simply taken off the schedule. You don't show up for golf and instead plan to do something else that you and your spouse agree to do enthusiastically.

But annoying habits are not planned. They seem to appear spontaneously. So if you want to rid yourself of those habits that seem to have a mind of their own, they require a different strategy that I will describe to you in the next chapter.

## Key Principles

**Annoying habits** are behaviors repeated without much thought that bother your spouse.

We persist in annoying habits because we don't feel what our spouse feels or we think that we should be accepted for who we are.

Whether it's intentional or not, our behavior will affect the love we have for each other.

The primary difference between an annoying habit and independent behavior is whether or not it's planned or part of a schedule. If it's planned, it's independent behavior. If it's an activity that is not planned or never was planned, it's an annoying habit.

## Consider This . . .

1. Are annoying habits a problem in your marriage? To answer that question, complete the annoying habits page (page 217) of the Love Busters Questionnaire in Appendix B. Make two enlarged

copies, one for each of you, so that you will have enough space to write your answers.

2. What is an annoying habit? I'm sure you have already overcome a few in your marriage. Can you think of things you've done in the past that were annoying to each other that are no longer an issue? How did you go about ridding yourselves of those Love Busters?

3. Most annoying habits are innocent—you don't do them to upset each other, it just turns out that way. Why can this make annoying habits more difficult to overcome than the other Love Busters we've discussed so far?

# 15

## Annoying Habits: *Part 2*

### How to Turn Annoying Habits into Pleasing Habits

Most of our annoying habits have a pleasing alternative. Instead of slouching in his chair, which was unattractive to Sharon, Mike could have learned the habit of sitting up straight, which she would have found attractive. By changing that one habit, Mike could have been making Love Bank deposits instead of withdrawals.

If you ever want to break a bad habit, the easiest way to do it is to find another behavior to take its place. As that new behavior is repeated whenever you would have engaged in the bad habit, you eliminate it with your new habit.

Anyone can turn annoying habits into pleasing ones if they have a good reason to do so. And your greatest motivation for change is the care you have for your spouse. If you want to avoid being the source of your spouse's unhappiness, and instead become the source of your spouse's happiness, you can do it by following these steps.

### Step 1: Identify each other's annoying habits.

The first step in solving most problems is to describe the problem, and that is certainly true when it comes to overcoming annoying habits. Both of you should make a list of as many as occur to you. While creating that list, you will be able to think of some of them almost immediately. But other habits will only occur to you when your spouse actually does them. So use your smartphone or get out a pad of paper that you keep close by, so you can add to your list when inspiration strikes. Take a few days to complete your inventory.

But as I mentioned in the last chapter, don't confuse annoying habits with the other Love Busters, especially independent behavior. While they might be annoying, the other Love Busters are defined differently, and require different strategies to overcome. So an annoying habit is not a selfish demand, a disrespectful judgment, an angry outburst, an independent behavior, or a lie.

Beside each annoying habit you list, enter a number between 1 and 10, indicating how intensely you are annoyed (1 = mildly annoying, 10 = extremely annoying). The numbers help identify the behavior that is making the largest Love Bank withdrawals.

When I ask a couple to list each other's annoying habits, the wife's list is almost always longer than the husband's list. In fact for many couples I counsel, the husbands have no entries at all. But it's not uncommon for a woman to list more than fifty habits she finds annoying.

I assure husbands that a long list of irritating behaviors should not lead them to conclude that they are incurably incompatible and that there is no hope. In fact, making the list is the first step toward improving compatibility—resolving problems that have been swept under a rug. They must uncover the dirt before they can vacuum it up.

And yet, this exercise has a high risk for hurt feelings. It's easy to think that your spouse's long list is an act of disrespect. But it's nothing of the kind. It's simply an honest reaction to habits that you can, and should, change.

But if you are not careful, you may actually be disrespectful when you make your lists. So go easy in the way you describe the annoying habits. Remember, most annoying habits are innocent—you just happen to find them annoying. The reason you want your spouse to change his or her habits is not necessarily because there is something wrong with the habits themselves. It's because they may prevent you from being in love.

I asked Sharon to let me see her list before she showed it to Mike. That's because I wanted to be sure that it did not contain any disrespectful comments. I wanted her descriptions of annoying habits to be simple and nonjudgmental. But she did not heed my advice. Her list still contained many comments such as "you should stop eating like a pig," and "stop being so sloppy and learn to pick up after yourself." After we weeded out her disrespectful judgments, the list described Mike's most annoying behavior respectfully.

Check your lists carefully before you show them to each other. Don't make the same mistakes that Sharon made when she made her first list. Instead, describe your spouse's annoying behavior as simply as possible, without making any value judgments about it. It annoys you, and that's all you need to explain. This was Sharon's list.

| Intensity Rating | Annoying Habits |
|---|---|
| 10 | Slouching in the living room chair |
| 7 | Tone of voice when disciplining the children |
| 8 | Overusing certain phrases, such as "you don't say" |
| 9 | Leaving toothpaste, toothbrush, shaver, and towel on the bathroom sink |
| 8 | Leaving clothes on the bedroom floor after getting ready for bed |
| 9 | Stuffing chips into mouth before swallowing the ones already there |
| 7 | Chewing ice and spitting it back into the glass |
| 8 | Picking teeth with finger after dinner |

### Step 2: Eliminate the easy ones first.

Each list of annoying habits usually includes a few habits that can be easily overcome with a simple decision to stop doing them. These are new habits that have not had time to become hardwired into your brain, or habits that do not provide much gratification.

But the one who is annoyed thinks all annoying habits should be easily overcome. Sharon thought that if she told Mike that the way he sat in the chair annoyed her, he could either stop doing it because he cared about her feelings, or he could keep doing it because he didn't care. It didn't occur to her that there was a third alternative—he cared about her feelings, but sat in an annoying way anyway because he was in the habit of doing so.

Sharon, like most people, did not understand the control habits have over us. She was under the illusion that we make a deliberate decision to do each thing we do. The truth is, most of what we do is automatic and effortless. One habit follows another and we really don't give much thought to what we do throughout the day.

Mike did not understand the control habits have over us either. He thought he could stop doing everything that Sharon listed with a simple decision to stop. But after we discussed each one with an eye to how long he had been doing it, and how much pleasure each gave him, we decided that picking his teeth with his finger might be Mike's easiest habit to overcome.

It turned out that we were right. Toothpicks were set by his plate, and he was encouraged to use them instead of his finger. He had not been using his finger to pick his teeth for long, it gave him very little pleasure, and the toothpicks were much easier for him to use. That made the old habit easy to replace with a new habit. So from that day on, Sharon never saw him do it again. But he knew that if she ever did, it would be re-entered onto her list.

If you can check off one or more annoying habits that you know will be easy to overcome, it will shorten the time it takes to eventually check them all off the list. But most habits take some time to change, so don't make the mistake of assuming that a simple decision to change is all it takes. And since most annoying habits are not easy to change, you shouldn't tackle too many annoying habits at once.

### Step 3: Select the three most annoying habits to overcome.

You can eventually eliminate most of each other's annoying habits, but to be successful I suggest that you should focus on no more than three at a time. Select the three behaviors that are the most annoying and eliminate those first.

After eliminating picking his teeth with his finger, it would have been tempting to work on all seven of the remaining habits to keep those Love Busters from doing any more damage. But I did not recommend that to Sharon and Mike. Instead, I suggested that they focus on the three habits that got her highest intensity ratings. If more than three had the same high rating, I would have suggested that Sharon select the three that she wanted to see overcome first.

On the list above, there was only one "10"—the way Mike sat on the chair in the living room. The next most annoying habits, "9s," were chip-stuffing and bathroom-messing. If there had been more 9s, Sharon would have picked the two that she wanted Mike to overcome first.

### Step 4: Create a plan to replace each annoying habit with a pleasing habit.

Whenever you create a plan to overcome a habit, remember that the habit is something you do almost unconsciously. The way you eat your cereal during breakfast, take a shower in the morning, and get into your car are instances of automatic, almost effortless habits. Over 95 percent of all you do is in the form of habits, because you really don't think about them, you simply do them. That's why some people think that habits should not be changed. They don't quite know how they acquired their habits and assume they're there for a good reason. But as it turns out, many of your habits are there for trivial reasons. It's the way you happened to do something at one point in time and you have just continued doing it that way ever since.

Habits are formed by simply repeating the new behavior often enough. Eventually you do it without giving it much thought. But if your spouse finds one of your habits to be annoying, it can be overcome by repeating another behavior in its place. It's a simple strategy that will work every time you try it.

There are two situations that you may face in trying to overcome an annoying habit.

1. You are able to change the conditions that trigger the habit, and learn a new pleasing habit under new triggering conditions, or
2. You must learn a new pleasing habit under the same conditions that trigger the old habit.

Of these two situations, the first, eliminating the conditions that trigger an annoying habit, is much easier to implement than changing the behavior under the influence of the existing conditions.

I'll give you an illustration of how changing habits in the first situation works.

Sharon was annoyed by the way Mike sat in the living room chair while watching television after he came home from work. But that wasn't the whole story. The slouching certainly annoyed her, but his entire homecoming routine bothered her, too. What she really wanted was his attention when he came home. So I created a plan that would solve both problems.

For Mike, the conditions of coming home from work and the placement of the chair and television were triggering conditions. His brain was wired to drive home after work, get out of his car, walk into the house, go straight to his favorite chair, grab the remote control, slouch, and then start watching TV.

My plan to help Mike overcome his annoying habit of slouching began by breaking up his entire homecoming routine. I suggested that when Mike came home from work each day, instead of going straight to the remote control, he spend about ten minutes sitting down with Sharon and a cup of coffee. They were to talk about how the day went and how they were planning to spend their evening. It helped break up his routine, which also changed the triggering conditions of his annoying behavior. And that made it easier to develop a new pleasing habit of how he would sit while he watched TV.

Just that one change made all the difference in the world. Since much of Sharon's irritability about how he sat in the chair had quite a bit to do with his finding the TV more interesting than her, his new routine changed all of that. Now he was focusing his attention on her instead of the TV.

But he was also sitting in his chair differently. Instead of slouching in his chair, Mike was sitting across from Sharon, back erect, talking to her about their days. He not only eliminated an annoying habit, replacing it with a pleasing habit, but he also replaced his entire homecoming routine. And in so doing, he met one of Sharon's important emotional needs: intimate conversation. Mike had a lot of love units to deposit, and talking to Sharon every day after work was a great way to start.

When it came time to watch TV with Sharon later in the evening, he had to practice sitting up straight there, too. So I encouraged Mike and Sharon to sit together on their loveseat. Prior to this assignment, they had been sitting apart from each other, with Sharon looking at the TV with one eye, and looking at Mike slouching in his chair with the other. When they were sitting together in a different chair, Sharon found that it didn't matter as much to her how Mike was sitting as long as it was beside her. But he still made an effort to sit up straight, and it was made easier by having a different place to sit.

Habits take a while to develop, so at first, Mike had to deliberately sit up straight, which made him feel a little uncomfortable. He tried various positions, but none were as comfortable as slouching.

Part of his discomfort was due to the fact that *any* new behavior can be uncomfortable at first. Whenever a new behavior is introduced to your brain, it must form new neural pathways before it feels natural to you. The more you repeat the new behavior, the more complete the new neural pathways become. Eventually, the pathways are completed, and you have a new habit—automatic and almost effortless.

I knew that Mike sat up straight in his chair at work and that didn't bother him, so he wasn't having a physical problem sitting that way. I suggested that he practice sitting the way Sharon wanted him to sit for just one week, to see how he would feel after doing it a few times.

For a few days Mike was uncomfortable coming home and finding that he could not sit in his chair and watch television right away. And he found that sitting down with his wife, talking about his day, was somewhat uncomfortable as well. Then, watching TV sitting beside Sharon was also uncomfortable at first. But after talking to Sharon after work and sitting the way Sharon wanted him to sit as they watched TV for just a few days, Mike agreed that it was becoming much more natural and comfortable for him.

The longer Mike practiced his new after-work and TV-watching routine, the more effortless it became. In fact, he eventually got to a point where he experienced quite a loss when Sharon was not there to greet him when he arrived home or sit with him when he watched TV. That's the way our habits work. When we're in the habit of doing something, we miss it if we're prevented from doing it.

The example I just used was based on the first situation that assumes that you can change the triggering conditions of the original annoying habit. We got rid of the chair, replaced it with a loveseat, and had Mike and Sharon sit beside each other. Those changes provided the opportunity for a new habit to be formed. But what if you are faced with the second situation where you can't eliminate the triggering conditions?

Suppose there were no other seating options in the room. And suppose that Sharon was not able to talk to Mike after work to break up his old habit of watching TV right away. How would you go about changing the behavior then? As it turns out, it's much more difficult to do, but it can also be done with dedication and persistence.

It takes a great deal more practice to change a habit when the triggering conditions can't be changed. It might have taken Mike weeks of sitting up straight if he had been faced with the same conditions. He would have had to deliberately practice his new sitting habit every night, and it might have been uncomfortable for a much longer period of time. That's why I encourage most couples to try to eliminate triggering conditions first if at all possible. But if the status quo causes unrelenting Love Bank Withdrawals, it's worth the effort to overcome annoying habits even when triggering conditions cannot be changed.

### Step 5: Measure your progress.

Whether a plan is easy or difficult to implement, it helps to document your progress. I encourage the couples I counsel to keep track of how things are going by writing any instance of the annoying habit on a sheet of paper. Of course, each record represents a failure to follow the plan. The date, time, and circumstances should also be documented. The spouse who finds the habit annoying should keep the record.

In completing this report, honesty is essential. An annoyed spouse might be tempted to go easy on their mate and under-report annoying incidents. Of course, this can undermine the entire process, and lead to no change in the habit. Even occasional failures can prevent a new habit from forming.

If a plan is followed perfectly, there is nothing to document. There are no failures. But if an annoying habit persists, I suggest changing the plan to eliminate it.

I don't consider a habit overcome until at least three months have passed with no failure. A phenomenon called "spontaneous recovery" can often cause the habit to mysteriously reappear months or even years after it seemed to end. But in such recurrences, the habit is no longer well-formed and can usually be overcome quickly by going right back to the original plan for its removal. Instead of months of practice, only days are required to resume the new habit.

### Step 6: Select the next three most annoying habits to overcome.

After you succeed at eliminating the three most annoying habits with a plan for each, you're ready to overcome the next three that are on the list. And you'll find that those will be much easier to overcome, because you now know the system for changing annoying habits into pleasing habits.

But at this point you may ask the question, *won't this turn out to be an endless task? Just as soon as I've eliminated all the annoying habits on the list, won't more come along? Am I going to be working on this the rest of my life?*

If you're following the Policy of Joint Agreement, where whatever you do must be with the mutual enthusiastic agreement of you and your spouse, any new annoying behavior simply won't ever be formed into habits. They'll never get off the ground. You may do something once or twice before you realize that it doesn't have your spouse's enthusiastic agreement, but that's not nearly enough repetitions for it to become a habit.

This procedure that I recommend to eliminate annoying habits may appear to be like using a sledgehammer to pound in a nail. But take it from an experienced psychologist: without a plan and a dedicated implementation of it, habits persist in spite of the best intentions to avoid them. That's why so many spouses eventually feel that it's useless to complain. All of their past complaints have been heard, and change was promised, but the annoying habits persist nonetheless.

Since almost everything you do affects each other, take your annoying habits very seriously. When you learn to overcome them, you will have eliminated one of the most insidious ways that spouses lose their love for each other. After you go to the trouble of changing a few habits, it will be just as easy for you to make your spouse happy as it was to make your spouse miserable.

Your annoying habits are not essential to your identity, and are certainly not inevitable. They are there for trivial reasons, and can be changed to make it just as effortless to make Love Bank deposits as it's been to make withdrawals. You'll be far more attractive to your spouse after those annoying habits have been transformed into pleasing habits.

## Key Principles

**Habits** are formed by simply repeating the new behavior often enough. Replace annoying habits with pleasing habits by following these steps:

1. Identify each other's annoying habits
2. Eliminate the easy ones first
3. Select the three most annoying habits to overcome
4. Create a plan to replace each annoying habit with a pleasing habit
5. Measure your progress
6. Select the next three most annoying habits to overcome

Any new behavior is often uncomfortable at first. Whenever a new behavior is introduced to your brain, it must form new neural pathways before it feels natural to you. But the more a new behavior is repeated, the stronger the new neural pathways become. Eventually, the pathways are completed, and a new habit is formed—automatic and almost effortless behavior.

Pleasing habits are just as effortless as annoying habits once they are formed.

## Consider This . . . ⸺

1. Does my plan to help you overcome annoying habits seem unnecessarily tedious? If it seems too overwhelming and prevents you from getting started, modify it enough that you will be willing to follow it for a while. But if you fail to eliminate annoying habits with your plan, agree to return to my plan, because I've found that it works whenever it's tried.
2. How does the Policy of Joint Agreement prevent the creation of new annoying habits?

# Bonus Chapter

## Building Romantic Love with Care

When Jo and Pete married, the most clearly understood part of their wedding vows was that they would care for each other throughout their lifetime. They understood that care is more than a feeling; it's a commitment to make every reasonable effort to meet each other's needs.

While they were still dating, Pete told Jo that if she married him he'd make her the happiest woman in history. She'd be the center of his life, and his world would revolve around her. Jo knew that if the marriage was to work she had to treat him the same way. She had to make him happy as well and make every effort to meet his needs.

They each had the right intentions and the correct understanding of care as a marital commitment. But they did not understand how difficult it would be to *learn* to care for each other. They both thought care was something you could decide to do, and once the decision was made, acts of care would be spontaneous.

But because their care for each other was not carefully planned, it fell far short of expectations. After they had been married for a few years, both Jo and Pete felt neglected.

Care is the *willingness* to change your own personal habits to meet the emotional needs of the person you have chosen to marry and then *making sure* that those habits are effective.

Care does not cause anyone to lose his or her identity or to become a robot. Our habits are often developed through chance and are not necessarily a reflection of our character or major goals in life. When we change them to accommodate our spouse's needs, we are actually controlling our behavior to fit our character.

But the process of discarding old habits and developing new ones can be difficult and stressful. This is one reason even well-intentioned couples often fail in their efforts to learn more accommodating habits. It's not only difficult for us to change for our spouse, but it is also difficult to put our spouse through the stress of making changes to accommodate us.

*Care is the willingness to change your own personal habits to meet the emotional needs of the person you have chosen to marry and then making sure that those habits are effective.*

Jo and Pete thought they were compatible when they were married. They got along with each other extremely well and felt that they were made for each other. It did not occur to them that after marriage new emotional needs would develop and prior acts of care would slowly fade away.

Care is more than learning to meet another's needs at a point in time and sustaining those habits; it also requires the willingness and ability to meet changing needs—adjusting to a moving target.

One of the more popular reasons for divorce today is that a husband and wife have "grown apart from each other." One of them may have completed an education, while the other did not. One may have developed a new career interest, and the other did not join in that interest. Very often children impact a couple's interests and send them in different directions.

But I believe that one of the most important reasons couples grow apart is that they fail to care for each other. Instead of continuing to meet emotional needs they met earlier in their marriage, they let new responsibilities distract them. And instead of learning how to meet new emotional needs that inevitably develop, couples assume that their instincts will carry them. Then when instinct seems to fail, they conclude that they must be incompatible.

Extramarital affairs or multiple divorces and remarriages represent one strategy in adjusting to the failure to create compatibility. Over a period of time, as emotional needs are unmet and a relationship falls apart, a new relationship is developed with another individual who is prepared to meet those needs.

If we were unable to continue meeting emotional needs that were met early in our romantic relationship, or to adjust to each other's changes in life, then I suppose multiple remarriages would be about the only solution to unsatisfactory relationships. But we have an enormous capacity for adjustment. Restoring our ability to meet each other's emotional needs and learning to meet each other's new needs is far less complicated than going through the agonizing ritual of divorce and remarriage.

If you want to have a successful and fulfilling marriage, you must care for each other by meeting each other's most important emotional needs. To achieve that objective, I recommend two essential steps: (1) discover what those needs are, and (2) learn to meet them.

## Step 1: Discover Your Spouse's Most Important Emotional Needs

The first step in learning to care for your spouse is discovering his or her emotional needs that exist today, and identifying those that are most important. Some of them might be the same as the ones you met for each other early in your marriage, while others may be entirely new.

An emotional need is a craving for something. When that need is met often enough, it makes you feel terrific (makes Love Bank deposits), but when it isn't met often enough, you feel frustrated.

There are thousands of emotional needs: peanut butter sandwiches, Monday night football, a cat in your lap, and a host of other things for which some people feel a craving. But which of those needs make the most Love Bank deposits when met? Those are the most important emotional needs.

Men and women usually have many of the same important emotional needs, but the *most* important can be very different. That can make the discovery of each other's most important emotional needs complex and difficult. Because husbands often try to meet needs most important to men and wives often try to meet needs most important to women, a couple can easily find themselves shooting at the wrong targets.

When the best efforts of a man and woman go unappreciated and their own most important emotional needs go unmet, they often give up trying. If they had only directed their efforts in the right places, they would have been appreciated and fulfilled.

My experience as a clinical psychologist has helped me identify ten of the most important emotional needs that can be met in marriage. While all ten are important, five tend to be of critical importance to most men, and the other five of critical importance to most women. These categories may not apply to either of you perfectly, but they can help you begin a discussion with each other to identify each other's most important emotional needs—the needs each of you should learn to meet.

A man's five most important needs in marriage tend to be:

1. *Sexual fulfillment.* A craving for sexual experiences. Enjoyment when the need is met often enough, and frustration when it is not. His wife meets this need by becoming a terrific sexual partner. She studies her own sexual response to recognize and understand what brings out the best in her; then she shares this information with him, and together they learn to have a sexual relationship that both find repeatedly satisfying and enjoyable.

2. *Recreational companionship.* A craving for recreational experiences with a companion. Enjoyment when the need is met often enough, and frustration when it is not. To meet his need, she develops an interest in the recreational activities he enjoys most and tries to become proficient at them. If she finds she cannot enjoy them, she encourages him to consider other activities that they can enjoy together. She becomes his favorite recreational companion, and he associates her with his most enjoyable moments of relaxation.

3. *Physical attractiveness.* A craving to view attractive people of the opposite sex. Enjoyment when the need is met often enough, and frustration when it is not. She meets that need by keeping herself physically fit with diet and exercise, and she wears her hair, makeup, and clothes in a way that he finds attractive and tasteful. He is attracted to her in private and proud of her in public.

4. *Domestic support.* A craving for a well-managed home. Enjoyment when the need is met often enough, and frustration when it is not. She meets his need by creating a home that offers him a refuge from the stresses of life. She manages household responsibilities in a way that encourages him to spend time at home enjoying his family.

5. *Admiration.* A craving to be admired, valued, and appreciated. Enjoyment when the need is met, and frustration when it is not. To meet his need, she understands and appreciates him more than anyone else. She reminds him of his value and achievements and helps him maintain self-confidence. She avoids criticizing him. She is proud of him, not out of duty, but from a profound respect for the man she chose to marry.

When a man is married to a woman who has learned to meet these needs, he'll find her irresistible. Love units are deposited into his Love Bank in such great numbers that he finds himself helplessly in love. That's because the fulfillment of these needs is essential to his happiness.

A woman's five most important needs in marriage tend to be:

1. *Affection.* A craving for affection. Enjoyment when the need is met often enough, and frustration when it is not. Her husband meets her need by telling her that he loves her with words, cards, flowers, gifts, and common courtesies. He hugs and kisses her many times each day, creating an environment of affection that clearly and repeatedly expresses his love for her.

2. *Conversation.* A craving for conversation. Enjoyment when the need is met often enough, and frustration when it is not. He meets her need by setting aside time every day to talk to her. They may talk about events in their lives, their children, their feelings, or their plans. But whatever the topic, she enjoys the conversation because it is never judgmental and always informative and constructive. She talks to him as much as she would like, and he responds with interest. He is never too busy "to just talk."

3. *Honesty and openness.* A craving for honesty and openness. Enjoyment when the need is met often enough, and frustration when it is not. Her need is met when he tells her everything about himself, leaving nothing out that might later surprise her. He describes his positive and negative feelings, events of his past, his daily schedule, and his plans for the future. He never leaves her with a false impression and is truthful about his thoughts, feelings, intentions, and behavior.

4. *Financial support.* A craving for financial support. Enjoyment when the need is met often enough, and frustration when it is not. He meets her need by assuming the responsibility to house, feed, and clothe his family. If his income is insufficient to provide essential support, he resolves the problem by upgrading his skills to increase his salary. He does not work long hours, keeping himself from his wife and family, but is able to provide necessary support by working a forty- to forty-five-hour week. While he encourages his wife to pursue a career, he does not depend on her salary for family living expenses.

5. *Family commitment.* A craving for family commitment. Enjoyment when the need is met often enough, and frustration when it is not. He meets her need by committing sufficient time and energy to the moral and educational development of the children. He reads to them, engages in sports with them, and takes them on frequent outings. He and his wife discuss training methods and objectives until they agree. He does not proceed with any plan of training or discipline without her approval. He recognizes that his care of the children is critically important to her.

When a woman is married to a man who has learned to meet these needs, she'll find him irresistible. Love units are deposited in her Love Bank in such great numbers that she finds herself helplessly in love. That's because the fulfillment of these needs is essential to her happiness.

Of course, *these categories do not apply to everyone.* Some men look at my "man's needs" list and throw two out to make room for two from my "woman's needs" list. Some women do the same. Believing that these categories are right for everyone is a big mistake!

I suggest reviewing these ten emotional needs to help you start the process of identifying what you need the most from each other. It is simply a way of helping you think through what makes you the happiest and most fulfilled. I also want you to realize that what a man needs in marriage is usually quite different from what a woman needs. That makes the whole process of discovering your needs very personal; it's something you must do for yourself. Then you should explain your discovery to your spouse.

To make this process more accurate and reliable, I suggest that you first pick one need from the ten. Pretend that, in your marriage, it's all you'll get. The other nine needs will *not* be met by your spouse. What need would you pick if you knew you would never get the rest? That's need number one.

Then do the same for need number two. If you will *not* get the other eight needs met by your spouse, what two would you pick? Continue this process until you've picked five. Those are likely to be the needs that you want your spouse to be particularly skilled in meeting for you.

Take a hard look at the needs you left behind. For example, if you did not include financial support, you should not expect your spouse to earn a dime! Are the needs you chose more important to you than financial support? How about physical attractiveness? If your spouse neglects his or her appearance, gains weight, or dresses carelessly, what would your emotional reaction be?

Some of my clients tell me that all ten are of critical importance. They could not survive a marriage that neglected any of them. But my experience has shown me that if only the top five emotional needs are met to the satisfaction of both spouses, the couple are in love with each other, and very satisfied with their marriage. On the other hand, if a couple tries to meet them all, they risk putting too little effort into meeting those that are most important. If you want to be in love with each other, meeting each other's *most important* emotional needs will do it.

## Step 2: Learn to Meet Your Spouse's Most Important Needs

Learning to meet your spouse's five most important marital needs usually requires literally hundreds, maybe thousands of new habits. But the habits all eventually come together to form a whole. It's like learning a part in a play: you begin by learning each line, each motion, each cue, but eventually it comes together. It's naturally whole; it doesn't seem like hundreds of little pieces.

To build the myriad of habits necessary to meet your spouse's needs, you must have a carefully planned strategy. *His Needs, Her Needs* provides a few strategies for you to consider for each of the ten needs. But the need for financial support may require you to consult a vocational counselor. The need for sexual fulfillment may require help from a sex therapist.

However you develop it, a strategy—a plan—should be created that has a good chance of improving your ability to meet the needs your spouse identified as most important.

Once you implement your plan, you may need someone to report to for accountability. Your spouse is the obvious choice, since he or she will know whether or not your plan is working. But if you find yourself to be too offended by your spouse's occasional negative feedback, a pastor or professional counselor may be better suited.

You have completed your plan when your spouse acknowledges its success—his or her emotional need is being met. But if, after all your effort, your spouse's needs are not being met, you must go back to the drawing board and plan a new strategy.

Honesty is essential at this stage of the program. If your plan does not meet your spouse's needs, it does neither of you any good to claim success.

But if you are successful, your spouse will tell you. You will see it in his or her eyes, and in the way your partner talks to you and responds to you. The "look of love" is unmistakable.

I view marriage as a profession. The skills I learn are designed to meet my spouse's most important emotional needs, and if I'm successful, she'll be in love with me. If she's not in love with me, I'm probably at fault and need to develop new skills. Of course, if I'm not in love with her and I've been honest about my feelings, it's her problem to solve.

As I've said earlier, *compatibility is created*. As a couple increases the number of habits that meet each other's marital needs, it improves their compatibility and their romantic love for each other.

We have such an opportunity in marriage to give each other exactly what we need. Many couples squander that opportunity. Don't let it happen to you!

# Bonus Chapter

## Building Romantic Love with Time

Before Jen and David were married, they spent the majority of their free time together. Her girlfriends knew that spending time with him was one of her highest priorities. So whenever they invited her somewhere, they knew she would be checking to see if she'd be missing an opportunity to be with him. On some occasions, she even broke dates with them if David had time to be with her.

David did the same. His friends didn't see nearly as much of him after he started dating Jen. And many of the things he had enjoyed doing were abandoned so that he could spend more time with her.

They tried to see each other on a daily basis. But on days when they couldn't get together, they called each other and sometimes talked for hours. Whether they were together in person or by phone, they gave each other their undivided attention.

The total amount of time they spent together in person or by phone in an average week was fifteen to twenty-five hours. But they weren't counting. They just took advantage of every opportunity.

After they were married, however, a change took place in the quality of their time together. They were actually with each other much more often but they spent less time giving each other undivided attention. David would come home and watch television all evening or play video games. Jen would be on the phone with her friends. Sometimes they would barely say a word to each other all evening. Then, after a few years of marriage, they were not even together very often. David would stay at work late into the night and Jen would plan to be with her friends evenings and weekends. As would be expected, the romance and feeling of love they once had for each other prior to marriage, didn't last very long.

Courtship is a custom that gives people a chance to prove that they can meet each other's emotional needs. If enough Love Bank deposits are made by meeting those needs, they fall in love with each other and marriage usually follows. But if a dating couple don't meet each other's emotional needs when they are together, or if they stop spending enough time together to meet those needs, the test fails and they end their relationship.

## The Policy of Undivided Attention

*Give your spouse your undivided attention a minimum of fifteen hours each week, using the time to meet the emotional needs of affection, sexual fulfillment, intimate conversation, and recreational companionship.*

But some, like David and Jen, spend enough time to prove that they can meet each other's emotional needs while dating, but after marriage, they stop meeting each other's emotional needs with the time they have together. And then, they eventually don't even spend much time with each other.

In the last chapter, I encouraged you to identify and then meet each other's five most important emotional needs. If you are like most couples, you may have discovered that the biggest barrier to your success was finding the time to do it. That's what I am up against when I am trying to help spouses fall in love with each other. If they want to be in love again, they must schedule time to do it.

So I've created a rule for couples that reminds them of the importance of scheduling time each week to meet some of each other's most important emotional needs. I call it the **Policy of Undivided Attention**: *Give your spouse your undivided attention a minimum of fifteen hours each week, using the time to meet the emotional needs of affection, sexual fulfillment, intimate conversation, and recreational companionship.*

It's incredible how many couples have tried to talk me out of the Policy of Undivided Attention. They begin by trying to convince me that it's impossible. Then they go on to the argument that it's impractical. Then they try to show me that it's impractical for *them*. But in the end, they usually agree that without time they cannot possibly achieve romantic love.

To help me explain how the Policy of Undivided Attention is to be applied in marriage, I've broken it down into three parts: privacy, objectives, and amount.

**1. Privacy:** *The time you plan to be together should not include children, relatives, or friends. Establish privacy so that you are able to give each other undivided attention.*

Why be alone? When you're alone as a couple, you have an opportunity to make the largest Love Bank deposits. When you're with others, everyone gets a little credit. Without privacy, romance in marriage can't survive. How successful would you have been dating each other if you didn't have privacy?

I recommend that couples learn to be without their children during these fifteen hours. I'm amazed at how difficult an assignment that is for some people. They don't regard their children as company! To them, an evening with their children is *privacy*. They think that the presence of their children prevents only lovemaking and they can do that after they go to bed. But I think the presence of children prevents much more than that: children keep the couple from focusing attention on each other, something desperately needed in marriage.

I also recommend that a couple learn not to include friends and relatives in the fifteen hours of time together. This may mean there's no time left over for friends and relatives. If that's the case, you're too busy, but at least you haven't sacrificed romance.

Finally, I teach couples what giving undivided attention means. Remember, it's what you did when you were dating. There's no way you would have married if you had ignored each other on dates. You looked at each other when you were talking, you were interested in the conversation, and there was little to distract you. This is the undivided attention you must give each other as a married couple.

When you see a movie, the time you're watching it doesn't count because you're not giving each other undivided attention. It's the same with television or sporting events. You should engage in these recreational activities, but your time together is to be very clearly defined: it's the time you pay close attention to each other.

Now that you're alone with each other, what should you do with this time? The second part of the Policy of Undivided Attention deals with objectives.

**2. Objectives:** *During this time, create activities that will meet your most important emotional needs: affection, sexual fulfillment, conversation, and recreational companionship.*

A painting is a good analogy in describing the Policy of Undivided Attention. The canvas is the time that you set aside to be alone with each other. But it's what you do with that time that makes it a beautiful painting or a big disappointment. Your goal should be to make that time the most enjoyable part of the week, just as it was for David and Jen when they were dating. And the way you can make it that enjoyable is to meet each other's emotional needs for affection, sexual fulfillment, conversation, and recreational companionship.

Romance for most men is sex and recreation; for women it's affection and conversation. When all four come together, men and women alike call it romance. That makes these categories somewhat inseparable for a date that men and women both enjoy. My advice is to combine them all, if you can, whenever you're alone with each other. That's what people do when they are in a romantic relationship. Why limit romance to novels and affairs?

Now for the final part of the policy. How *much* time do you need?

**3. Amount:** *Choose a number of hours that reflects the quality of your marriage. If your marriage is satisfying to you and your spouse, plan fifteen hours. But if you suffer marital dissatisfaction, plan more hours each week until marital satisfaction is achieved. Keep a permanent record of your time together.*

How much time do you need to sustain romance? Believe it or not, there really is an answer to this question, and it depends on the health of a marriage. If a couple is deeply in love with each other and finds that their marital needs are being met, I have found that about fifteen hours each week of undivided attention is usually enough to sustain a romantic marriage. It is probably the least amount of time necessary. When a marriage is this healthy, either it's a new marriage or the couple has already been spending fifteen hours a week alone with each other throughout their marriage.

When I apply the fifteen-hour principle to marriages, I usually recommend that the time be evenly distributed through the week, two to three hours each day. When time must be bunched up, all hours on the weekend, good results are not as predictable. People seem to need intimacy almost on a daily basis.

For couples on the verge of divorce or entangled in an affair, I recommend much more time. In some cases, I have advised couples to take a leave of absence from work and other responsibilities, go on a vacation, and spend the entire time restoring intimacy that had been lost over the years.

It's always been a mystery to me how workaholic businessmen find time to have an affair. The man who can't be home for dinner is scheduling mid-afternoon adventures three times a week. How does he get his work done? The answer, of course, is that he had the time all along. It's simply a matter of priorities. He could just as easily have taken time to be with his wife. Then he would have been madly in love with her instead of his secretary.

The reason I have so much difficulty getting couples to spend time alone together is that they're not in love. Their relationship doesn't do anything for them, and the time spent together seems a total waste at first. But with that time they can learn to re-create the romantic experiences that first brought them together in a love relationship. Without that time, they have little hope of restoring the love they once had for each other.

Whether your marriage needs fifteen hours a week or more than that, remember that the time spent is only equivalent to a part-time job. It isn't time you don't have; it's time you've filled with something less important.

To help couples get into the habit of scheduling time alone, I have encouraged them to make a chart, keeping track of the number of hours alone each week. Each person independently estimates the time actually spent giving undivided attention, and the number entered on the chart should be the lower of the two estimates.

This chart becomes an excellent predictor of marital fulfillment. It's like the Index of Leading Economic Indicators for marital health. During periods when a couple spends a large number of hours alone together, they can look forward in future months to a very warm and intimate love relationship. But when the chart shows that very few hours have been spent together, the couple can expect to find themselves arguing more often and feeling less fulfilled in the months ahead.

I also encourage both husband and wife to use their smartphone or appointment book to remind them of their scheduled time together. Here they document the time they've set aside to be with each other. While I'm counseling them, I make certain that they keep the dates they set for each other and that they are always recorded.

Since we are creatures of habit, I recommend that the hours spent alone be at the same time each day and the same day week after week. You will probably be able to schedule more time together on the weekends. If you keep the same schedule every week, it will be easier to follow the Policy of Undivided Attention than if you change it every week.

Remember, the total amount of time you spend together doesn't necessarily affect the way you feel about each other in the week that the time was spent. It has more effect on the way you're *going to feel* about each other in future weeks. You're building Love Bank accounts when you spend time together, and the account must build before you feel the effect.

From my perspective as a marriage counselor, the time you spend alone with each other is the most valuable of your week. It's the time when you are depositing the most love units and ensuring romantic love for your marriage.

# Appendix A

# Basic Concepts to Help You Fall in Love and Stay in Love

If you apply all of my Basic Concepts to your marriage, you will do what most couples want to do, but have failed to do—fall in love and stay in love. And that's what ultimately saves marriage— restoring the feeling of love. I've never counseled a couple in love that want to divorce.

When you are in love, your emotions help you meet each other's emotional needs. They provide instincts that you may not have even known you have—instincts to be affectionate, sexual, conversational, recreational, honest, and admiring. These all seem to come naturally when you are in love.

But life can throw roadblocks across your path to marital bliss. The demands of a job or even children can limit your opportunity to meet each other's emotional needs. When that happens, very innocently and without any intent, you stop caring for each other as you had in the past, and you fall out of love.

When you fall out of love, everything that had helped your marriage seems unnatural. Your instincts turn against marital recovery and toward divorce. What had once seemed effortless now seems awkward. How can you restore the love you once had for each other when you no longer feel like doing what it took to create that love?

I've created these Basic Concepts to help you answer that question—to help you do what it takes to restore your love for each other when you are not in love, when you don't feel like doing any of them. And then once your love is restored, these concepts will help you stay in love for the rest of your lives.

## Basic Concept 1: The Love Bank

In my struggle to learn how to save marriages, I discovered that the best way to do it was to teach couples how to fall in love—and stay in love—with each other. So I created the concept of the Love Bank to help couples understand how people fall in and out of love. This concept, perhaps more than any other that I have created, has helped couples realize that almost everything they do affects their love for each other either positively or negatively. That awareness has set most of them on a course of action that has preserved their love and saved their marriages.

Within each of us is a Love Bank that tracks the way people treat us. Everyone you know has an account in your Love Bank, and the things they do either deposit or withdraw love units from their accounts. It's the way your emotions encourage you to be with those who make you happy. When you associate someone with good feelings, deposits are made into that person's account in your Love Bank. And when the Love Bank reaches a certain level of deposits (the romantic love threshold), the feeling of love is triggered. As long as your Love Bank balance remains above that threshold, you will experience the feeling of love. But when it falls below that threshold, you will lose that feeling. You will like anyone with a balance above zero, but you will only be in love with someone whose balance is above the romantic love threshold.

Not only do your emotions encourage you to be with those who make you happy, they also discourage you from being with those who make you unhappy. Whenever you associate someone with bad feelings, withdrawals are made from your Love Bank. And if that person makes more withdrawals than deposits, his or her balance in your Love Bank can fall below zero. When that happens the Love Bank turns into the Hate Bank. You will dislike those with moderate negative balances, but if a balance falls below the hate threshold, you will hate the person.

Try living with a spouse you hate! Your emotions are doing everything they can to get you out of there—and divorce is one of the most logical ways to escape.

Couples usually ask for my advice when they are just about ready to give up on their marriage. Their Love Banks have been losing love units for so long that they are now deeply in the red. And their negative Love Bank accounts make them feel uncomfortable just being in the same room with each other. They cannot imagine surviving marriage for another year, let alone ever being in love again.

But that's my job—to help them fall in love with each other again. I encourage them to stop making Love Bank withdrawals and start making Love Bank deposits. I created all of the remaining basic concepts to help couples achieve those objectives.

## Basic Concept 2: Instincts and Habits

Instincts are behavioral patterns that we are born with, and habits are patterns that we learn. Both instincts and habits tend to be repeated again and again almost effortlessly. They are important in our discussion of what it takes to be in love because it's our behavior that makes deposits in and withdrawals from Love Banks, and our instincts and habits make up most of our behavior.

Instincts and habits can make Love Bank deposits, so it is imperative to learn those habits because once they are learned, deposits in your spouse's Love Bank are made repeatedly and almost effortlessly.

Unfortunately, many of our instincts and habits, such as angry outbursts, contribute to Love Bank withdrawals. Since they are repeated so often, they play a very important role in the annihilation of Love Bank accounts. If we are to stop Love Bank withdrawals, we must somehow stop destructive instincts and habits in their tracks. Instincts are harder to stop than habits, but they can both be avoided.

203

As we discuss the remaining concepts, keep in mind the value of a good habit and the harm of a bad habit, because their effect on Love Bank balances is multiplied by repetition.

## Basic Concept 3: The Most Important Emotional Needs

What's the fastest way to deposit love units into each other's Love Banks? I interviewed literally hundreds of couples trying to find the answer to this question when I was first learning how to save marriages. Eventually the answer became clear to me—you must meet each other's most important emotional needs.

You and your spouse fell in love with each other because you made each other very happy, and you made each other happy because you met some of each other's important emotional needs. The only way you and your spouse will stay in love is if you keep meeting those needs. Even when the feeling of romantic love begins to fade, or when it's gone entirely, it's not necessarily gone for good. It can be recovered whenever you both go back to making large Love Bank deposits.

Your spouse depends on you to meet his or her most important emotional needs, and it's the most effective and efficient way for you to make large deposits in your spouse's Love Bank.

## Basic Concept 4: The Policy of Undivided Attention

Unless you and your spouse schedule time each week for undivided attention, it will be impossible to meet each other's most important emotional needs. To help you and your spouse clear space in your schedule for each other, I have written the **Policy of Undivided Attention**: *Give your spouse your undivided attention for a minimum of fifteen hours each week, using the time to meet the emotional needs of affection, sexual fulfillment, conversation, and recreational companionship.* This policy will help you avoid one of the most common mistakes in marriage—neglecting each other.

This basic concept not only helps guarantee that you will meet each other's emotional needs but also unlocks the door to the use of all the other basic concepts. Without time for undivided attention, you will not be able to avoid Love Busters and you will not be able to negotiate effectively. Time for undivided attention is the necessary ingredient for everything that's important in marriage.

And yet, as soon as most couples marry, and especially when children arrive, couples usually replace their time together with activities of lesser importance. You probably did the same thing. You tried to meet each other's needs with "leftover" time, but sadly, there wasn't much time left over. Your lack of private time together may have become a great cause of unhappiness, and yet you felt incapable of preventing it. You may have also found yourself bottling up your honest expression of feelings because there was just no appropriate time to talk.

### Policy of Undivided Attention

*Give your spouse your undivided attention for a minimum of fifteen hours each week, using the time to meet the emotional needs of affection, sexual fulfillment, conversation, and recreational companionship.*

Make your time to be alone with each other your highest priority—that way it will never be replaced by activities of lesser value. Your career, your time with your children, maintenance of your home, and a host of other demands will all compete for your time together. But if you follow the Policy of Undivided Attention, you will not let anything steal away those precious and crucial hours together.

It is essential to (a) spend time away from children and friends whenever you give each other your undivided attention; (b) use the time to meet each other's emotional needs of affection, conversation, recreational companionship, and sexual fulfillment; and (c) schedule at least fifteen hours together each week. When you were dating, you gave each other this kind of attention and you fell in love. When people have affairs, they also give each other this kind of attention to keep their love for each other alive. Why should courtship and affairs be the only times love is created? Why can't it happen throughout marriage as well? It can, if you set aside time every week to give each other undivided attention.

## Basic Concept 5: Love Busters

When you meet each other's most important emotional needs, you become each other's source of greatest happiness. But if you are not careful, you can also become each other's source of greatest unhappiness.

It's pointless to deposit love units if you withdraw them right away. So, in addition to meeting important emotional needs, you must also be sure to protect your spouse. Guard your account in your spouse's Love Bank from withdrawals by paying attention to how your everyday behavior can make each other unhappy.

You and your spouse were born to be demanding, disrespectful, angry, dishonest, independent, and annoying. These are normal human traits that I call Love Busters because they destroy the feeling of love spouses have for each other. But if you promise to avoid being the cause of your spouse's unhappiness, you will do whatever it takes to overcome these destructive tendencies for your spouse's protection. By eliminating Love Busters, you will not only be protecting your spouse, but you will also be preserving your spouse's love for you.

## Basic Concept 6: The Policy of Radical Honesty

If you and your spouse are to be in love with each other, you must give honesty special attention. That's because it plays such an important role in the creation of love. It is one of the ten most important emotional needs, so when it's met, it can trigger the feeling of love. On the other hand, its counterpart, dishonesty, is a Love Buster—it destroys love.

But there is another reason that honesty is crucial in creating love. Honesty is the only way that you and your spouse will ever come to understand each other. Without honesty, the adjustments that are crucial to making each other happy and avoiding unhappiness cannot be made.

It isn't easy to be honest. Honesty is an unpopular value these days, and most couples have not made this commitment to each other. Many marriage counselors and even clergymen argue that honesty is not always the best policy. They believe that it's cruel to disclose past indiscretions and it's selfish to make such disclosures. While it makes you feel better to get a mistake off your chest, it causes your partner to suffer. So, they argue, the truly caring thing to do is to lie about your mistakes or at least keep them tucked away.

And if it's compassionate to lie about sins of the past, why isn't it also compassionate to lie about sins of the present—or future? To my way of thinking, it's like letting the proverbial camel's nose under the tent. Eventually you will be dining with the camel. Either honesty is always right, or you'll always have an excuse for being dishonest.

To help remind couples how important honesty is in marriage, I have written the **Policy of Radical Honesty:** *Reveal to your spouse as much information about yourself as you know—your thoughts, feelings, habits, likes, dislikes, personal history, daily activities, and plans for the future.*

> ## Policy of Radical Honesty
>
> *Reveal to your spouse as much information about yourself as you know—your thoughts, feelings, habits, likes, dislikes, personal history, daily activities, and plans for the future.*

Self-imposed honesty with your spouse is essential to your marriage's safety and success. Not only will honesty bring you closer to each other emotionally, it will also prevent the creation of destructive habits that are kept secret from your spouse.

## Basic Concept 7: The Policy of Joint Agreement

Marital instincts do not lead to fair negotiation. They lead to either giving away the store when you are feeling generous or robbing the bank when feeling selfish. And when in withdrawal, no one even feels like negotiating. Yet in order to meet each other's most important needs and avoid Love Busters consistently and effectively, fair negotiation is crucial in marriage.

So you need a rule to help you remember to be fair when you negotiate so that both of you win. I call this rule the **Policy of Joint Agreement:** *Never do anything without an enthusiastic agreement between you and your spouse.*

Almost everything you and your spouse do affects each other. So it's very important to know what that effect will be before you actually do it. The Policy of Joint Agreement will help you remember to consult with each other to be sure you avoid being the cause of each other's unhappiness. It also makes negotiation necessary, regardless of your state of mind. If you agree to this policy, you will not be able to do anything without the enthusiastic agreement of the other, so it forces you to discuss your plans and negotiate with each other's feelings in mind. Without safe and pleasant negotiation, you will simply not be able to reach an enthusiastic agreement.

> **Policy of Joint Agreement**
>
> *Never do anything without an enthusiastic agreement between you and your spouse.*

The Policy of Joint Agreement, combined with the Policy of Radical Honesty, helps you create an open and integrated lifestyle, one that will guarantee your love for each other. These policies also prevent the creation of a secret second life where infidelity, the greatest threat to your marriage, can grow like mold in a damp, dark cellar.

### Basic Concept 8: Four Guidelines for Successful Negotiation in Marriage

If you and your spouse are in conflict about anything, I recommend that you do nothing until you can both agree enthusiastically about a resolution. But how should you go about reaching that resolution? I suggest you follow four essential guidelines.

#### Guideline 1: Set ground rules to make negotiation pleasant and safe.

*Ground rule 1* Try to be pleasant and cheerful throughout negotiations.

*Ground rule 2* Put safety first. Do not make demands, show disrespect, or become angry when you negotiate, even if your spouse makes demands, shows disrespect, or becomes angry with you.

*Ground rule 3*   If you reach an impasse and you do not seem to be getting anywhere, or if one of you is starting to make demands, show disrespect, or become angry, stop negotiating and come back to the issue later.

### Guideline 2: Identify the problem from both perspectives.

Be sure to show mutual respect for those perspectives.

### Guideline 3: Brainstorm with abandon.

Give your creativity a chance to discover solutions that would make you both happy. Jot down ideas as you think of them throughout the day.

### Guideline 4: Choose the solution that best meets the conditions of the Policy of Joint Agreement—mutual and enthusiastic agreement.

Whenever a conflict arises, keep in mind the importance of finding a solution that deposits as many love units as possible, while avoiding withdrawals. And be sure that the way you find that solution also deposits love units and avoids withdrawals.

# Appendix B

# Love Busters Questionnaire

© 1992, 2013, 2016 by Willard F. Harley, Jr.

Name _____ Date _____

This questionnaire is designed to help identify your spouse's Love Busters. Your spouse engages in a Love Buster whenever one of his or her habits causes you to be unhappy. By causing your unhappiness, your spouse withdraws love units from your Love Bank, and that, in turn, threatens your romantic love for him or her.

There are six categories of Love Busters. Each category has its own set of questions in this questionnaire. Answer all the questions as candidly as possible. Do not try to minimize your unhappiness with your spouse's behavior. If your answers require more space, use and attach a separate sheet of paper.

When you have completed this questionnaire, go through it a second time to be certain your answers accurately reflect your feelings. Do not erase your original answers, but cross them out lightly so that your spouse can see the corrections and discuss them with you.

When you have completed this questionnaire, rank the six Love Busters in order of their importance to you. When you have finished ranking the Love Busters, you may find that your answers to the questions regarding each Love Buster are inconsistent with your final ranking. This inconsistency is common. It often reflects a less-than-perfect understanding of your feelings. If you notice inconsistencies, discuss them with your spouse to help clarify your feelings.

You have the permission of the publisher to photocopy the questionnaire, enlarging to 8½ × 11, for use in your own marriage.

**1. Selfish Demands:** Attempts by your spouse to force you to do something for him or her that benefits your spouse at your expense.

**A. Selfish Demands as a Cause of Unhappiness:** Indicate how much unhappiness you tend to experience when your spouse makes selfish demands of you.

```
0        1        2        3        4        5        6
|_____|_____|_____|_____|_____|_____|
I experience                I experience              I experience
no unhappiness              moderate unhappiness       extreme unhappiness
```

**B. Frequency of Spouse's Selfish Demands:** Indicate how often your spouse makes selfish demands of you.

_____ selfish demands each day/week/month/year.
(write number)                              (circle one)

**C. Form(s) Selfish Demands Take:** When your spouse makes selfish demands of you, what does he or she typically do?

_____

_____

**D. Form of Selfish Demands That Causes the Greatest Unhappiness:** Which of the above forms of selfish demands causes you the greatest unhappiness?

_____

_____

**E. Onset of Selfish Demands:** When did your spouse first make selfish demands of you?

_____

_____

**F. Development of Selfish Demands:** Have your spouse's selfish demands increased or decreased in intensity and/or frequency since they first began? How do recent selfish demands compare to those of the past?

_____

_____

2. **Disrespectful Judgments:** Attempts by your spouse to change your attitudes, beliefs, and behavior through lecture, ridicule, threats, or any other forceful means.

   A. **Disrespectful Judgments as a Cause of Unhappiness:** Indicate how much unhappiness you tend to experience when your spouse engages in disrespectful judgments toward you.

   | 0 | 1 | 2 | 3 | 4 | 5 | 6 |
   |---|---|---|---|---|---|---|

   I experience
   no unhappiness

   I experience
   moderate unhappiness

   I experience
   extreme unhappiness

   B. **Frequency of Spouse's Disrespectful Judgments:** Indicate how often your spouse tends to engage in disrespectful judgments toward you.

   _____ disrespectful judgments each day/week/month/year.

   (write number)                                     (circle one)

   C. **Form(s) Disrespectful Judgments Take:** When your spouse engages in disrespectful judgments toward you, what does he or she typically do?

   _____

   _____

   D. **Form of Disrespectful Judgments That Causes the Greatest Unhappiness:** Which of the above forms of disrespectful judgments causes you the greatest unhappiness?

   _____

   _____

   E. **Onset of Disrespectful Judgments:** When did your spouse first engage in disrespectful judgments toward you?

   _____

   _____

   F. **Development of Disrespectful Judgments:** Have your spouse's disrespectful judgments increased or decreased in intensity and/or frequency since they first began? How do recent disrespectful judgments compare to those of the past?

   _____

**3. Angry Outbursts:** Deliberate attempts by your spouse to hurt you because of anger toward you. They are usually in the form of verbal or physical attacks.

  **A. Angry Outbursts as a Cause of Unhappiness:** Indicate how much unhappiness you tend to experience when your spouse attacks you with an angry outburst.

```
0        1        2        3        4        5        6
|        |        |        |        |        |        |
I experience          I experience              I experience
no unhappiness        moderate unhappiness      extreme unhappiness
```

  **B. Frequency of Spouse's Angry Outbursts:** Indicate how often your spouse tends to engage in angry outbursts toward you.

    _____ angry outbursts each day/week/month/year.
    (write number)                    (circle one)

  **C. Form(s) Angry Outbursts Take:** When your spouse engages in angry outbursts toward you, what does he or she typically do?

  _____

  _____

  **D. Form of Angry Outbursts That Causes the Greatest Unhappiness:** Which of the above forms of angry outbursts causes you the greatest unhappiness?

  _____

  _____

  **E. Onset of Angry Outbursts:** When did your spouse first engage in angry outbursts toward you?

  _____

  _____

  **F. Development of Angry Outbursts:** Have your spouse's angry outbursts increased or decreased in intensity and/or frequency since they first began? How do recent angry outbursts compare to those of the past?

  _____

  _____

4. **Dishonesty:** Failure of your spouse to reveal his or her thoughts, feelings, habits, likes, dislikes, personal history, daily activities, and plans for the future. Dishonesty is not only providing false information about any of the above topics, but it is also leaving you with what he or she knows is a false impression.

   A. **Dishonesty as a Cause of Unhappiness:** Indicate how much unhappiness you tend to experience when your spouse is dishonest with you.

   ```
   0        1        2        3        4        5        6
   ```

   | | | |
   |---|---|---|
   | I experience no unhappiness | I experience moderate unhappiness | I experience extreme unhappiness |

   B. **Frequency of Spouse's Dishonesty:** Indicate how often your spouse tends to be dishonest with you.

   _____ instances of dishonesty each day/week/month/year.
   (write number)                                          (circle one)

   C. **Form(s) Dishonesty Takes:** When your spouse is dishonest with you, what does he or she typically do?

   _____

   _____

   D. **Form of Dishonesty That Causes the Greatest Unhappiness:** Which of the above forms of dishonesty causes you the greatest unhappiness?

   _____

   _____

   E. **Onset of Dishonesty:** When was your spouse first dishonest with you?

   _____

   _____

   F. **Development of Dishonesty:** Has your spouse's dishonesty increased or decreased in intensity and/or frequency since it first began? How do recent instances of dishonesty compare to those of the past?

   _____

   _____

215

**5. Independent Behavior:** Behavior conceived and executed by your spouse without consideration of your feelings. These behaviors are usually scheduled and require thought to complete, such as attending sporting events or engaging in a personal exercise program.

**A. Independent Behavior as a Cause of Unhappiness:** Indicate how much unhappiness you tend to experience when your spouse engages in independent behavior.

```
0        1        2        3        4        5        6
|--------|--------|--------|--------|--------|--------|
I experience          I experience           I experience
no unhappiness        moderate unhappiness   extreme unhappiness
```

**B. Frequency of Spouse's Independent Behavior:** Indicate how often your spouse tends to engage in independent behavior.

_____ occurrences of independent behavior each day/week/month/year.

(write number)                                                 (circle one)

**C. Form(s) Independent Behavior Takes:** When your spouse engages in independent behavior toward you, what does he or she typically do?

_____

_____

**D. Form of Independent Behavior That Causes the Greatest Unhappiness:** Which of the above forms of independent behavior causes you the greatest unhappiness?

_____

_____

**E. Onset of Independent Behavior:** When did your spouse first engage in independent behavior?

_____

_____

**F. Development of Independent Behavior:** Has your spouse's independent behavior increased or decreased in intensity and/or frequency since it first began? How does recent independent behavior compare to that of the past?

_____

_____

6. **Annoying Habits:** Behavior repeated by your spouse without much thought that bothers you. These habits include personal mannerisms such as the way your spouse eats, cleans up after him- or herself, and talks.

   A. **Annoying Habits as a Cause of Unhappiness:** Indicate how much unhappiness you tend to experience when your spouse engages in annoying habits.

   0     1     2     3     4     5     6

   I experience no unhappiness     I experience moderate unhappiness     I experience extreme unhappiness

   B. **Frequency of Spouse's Annoying Habits:** Indicate how often your spouse tends to engage in annoying habits.

   _____ occurrences of annoying habits each day/week/month/year.

   (write number)     (circle one)

   C. **Form(s) Annoying Habits Takes:** When your spouse engages in annoying habits toward you, what does he or she typically do?

   _____

   _____

   D. **Form of Annoying Habits That Causes the Greatest Unhappiness:** Which of the above forms of annoying habits causes you the greatest unhappiness?

   _____

   _____

   E. **Onset of Annoying Habits:** When did your spouse first engage in annoying habits?

   _____

   _____

   F. **Development of Annoying Habits:** Have your spouse's annoying habits increased or decreased in intensity and/or frequency since they first began? How do those recent annoying habits compare to those of the past?

   _____

   _____

# Ranking Love Busters

The six basic categories of Love Busters are listed below. There is also space for you to add other categories of Love Busters that you feel contribute to your marital unhappiness. In the space provided in front of each Love Buster, write a number from 1 to 6 that ranks its relative contribution to your unhappiness. Write a 1 before the Love Buster that causes you the greatest unhappiness, a 2 before the one causing the next greatest unhappiness, and so on, until you have ranked all six.

_____ Selfish Demands

_____ Disrespectful Judgments

_____ Angry Outbursts

_____ Dishonesty

_____ Independent Behavior

_____ Annoying Habits

\_\_\_\_\_ _____

\_\_\_\_\_ _____

Dr. Willard F. Harley, Jr., is a nationally acclaimed clinical psychologist, marriage counselor, and bestselling author. His popular website, MarriageBuilders.com, offers practical solutions to almost any marital problem. He and Joyce, his wife of over fifty years, host a daily radio call-in show, *Marriage Builders Radio*. They live in White Bear Lake, Minnesota.

# The best book on marriage is now *better than ever!*

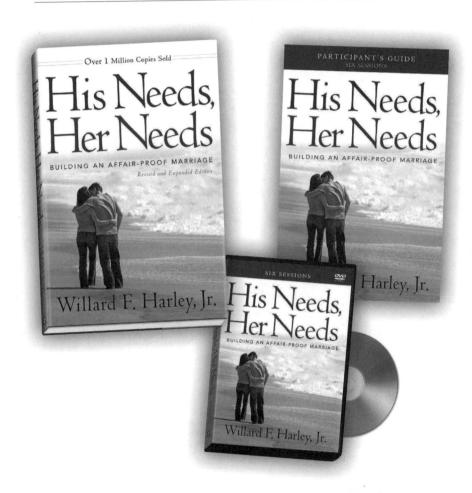

For over twenty-five years, *His Needs, Her Needs* has been transforming marriages all over the world. Now this life-changing book is the basis for an interactive six-week DVD study designed for use in couples' small groups or retreats, in premarital counseling sessions, or by individual couples.

# Take the next step to strengthen your marriage.

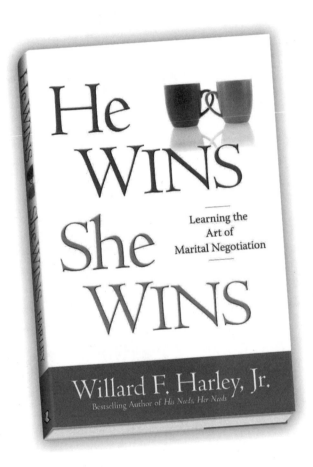

Through the process of "joint agreement," you and
your spouse can make decisions together and both get
what you want and believe is best—*every time*.

ℛ Revell
*a division of Baker Publishing Group*
www.RevellBooks.com

Available wherever books and ebooks are sold.  f  🐦

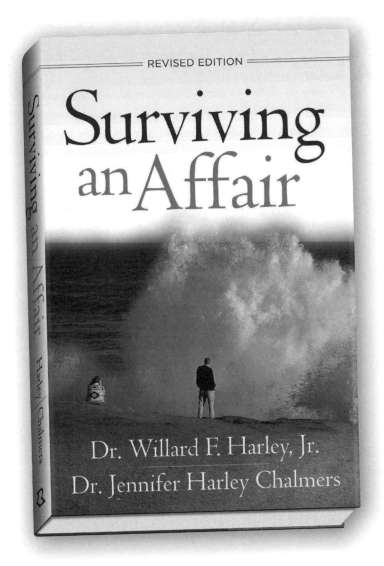

# MARRIAGE BUILDERS

### *Building Marriages To Last A Lifetime*

At MarriageBuilders.com, Dr. Harley introduces you to the best ways to overcome marital conflicts and the quickest ways to restore love.

Read Dr. Harley's articles, follow the Q&A columns, interact with other couples on the Forum, and listen to Dr. Harley and his wife, Joyce, answer your questions on Marriage Builders® Radio. Learn to become an expert in making your marriage the best it can be.

*Let Marriage Builders® help you build a marriage to last a lifetime!*

**www.marriagebuilders.com**